P9-DGM-795

DAILY WORD

Love, Inspiration, and Guidance for Everyone

Daybreak™ Books
A Division of Rodale Press, Inc.
Emmaus, Pennsylvania

Daybreak is a trademark of Rodale Press, Inc.

Printed in the United States of America on acid-free (∞), recycled paper ♻

Cover Designer: Barbara Scott-Goodman
Cover and Interior Illustrator: Vicki Wehrman

Library of Congress Cataloging-in-Publication Data

Zuck, Colleen.
    Daily Word: love, inspiration, and guidance for everyone / by Colleen
Zuck.
        p.   cm.
    Includes index.
    ISBN 0–87596–442–7 hardcover
    1. Devotional calendars.   I. Title.
BV4810.Z83 1997
242'.2—dc21   96–29601

Distributed in the book trade by St. Martin's Press

    4   6   8   10   9   7   5   3   hardcover

OUR PURPOSE

*"We publish books that empower
people's minds and spirits."*

ACKNOWLEDGMENTS

This book was truly a team effort, made possible only through the dedication and talent of the *Daily Word* staff: Janie Wright, associate editor; Elaine Meyer, assistant editor; and Linda Kahler, editorial assistant.

Their commitment to excellence and to sharing the beauty of their souls, along with the devoted work of Chris Jackson, consulting editor, has made this book possible.

—Colleen Zuck

FOREWORD
BY FANNIE FLAGG

When I was asked if I would write a few words for this book, I was thrilled and flattered. "No problem," I said, thinking of everything but the moment when I would actually sit down and begin to write. Well, that moment has arrived.

I know exactly how I feel about *Daily Word*, but how will I ever be able to get it down on paper? What words could I possibly use that would accurately describe what *Daily Word* means to me and to millions of others around the world?

Regular readers of *Daily Word* magazine will already know what a joy and comfort this book will be for them, but how can I—without sounding overly dramatic or making such a fool of myself that you run screaming out of the bookstore—tell a new reader who is discovering *Daily Word* and this book for the first time?

What I can do is tell you how *Daily Word* literally changed my life, and believe me, I was a hard case. My first copy of *Daily Word* magazine came to me in 1967. A friend sent me a subscription, and, quite honestly, I was annoyed. My immediate thought was, "Oh no, not another bunch trying to push religion down my throat." And so each month *Daily Word* came, and each month I threw it out. Until one day, for some unknown reason, I picked it up and read it, and I was totally surprised! *Daily Word* isn't of any one religion; it doesn't even suggest that one religion is the right one or the wrong one. It is about spirituality, embracing all types of beliefs and schools of thought. It is written not just for some, but for everyone, reminding us that we are children of God, that we are never alone, and that God wants us to be happy, free, and to enjoy life! Wow, what a concept!

I was attracted by the gentle and simple way it was written, and I still am. When I was going through dark and unhappy days and needed help, I was amazed to find that each day's message seemed to say just what I needed to hear, to offer me just the right answer. One of the many miracles of being human is that although we all are incredibly different and unique from one another, there is a part of us that is exactly the same. When the first person who ever lived asked the very first question, I'll bet the question was: "Is anybody out there? Does anybody know I'm here? Does anybody care?" And over the years, *Daily Word*'s answer has been *yes*.

Reading *Daily Word* every morning continues to be so important. Like you, perhaps, I forget where I put my keys, my glasses, my purse, and yes, even my *Daily Word*. And I can just as easily get distracted by life and forget who I am and that God loves me. I can even forget there is a God. *Daily Word* reminds me that even though the world around me may be changing, God never changes. And when I wake up feeling depressed, scared, or lonely, it is my way to get over to the sunny side of the street, to start my day with a positive thought. Most of us have someone we know who loves us, someone we call just to hear that familiar voice, just to check in with them to see if they are still there and still love us. That is what *Daily Word* has come to be for so many of us.

So whether you are a new reader or an old friend, I know each day you will read the exact words you need to hear and no matter what time you read it, night or day, there will be thousands who will be reading the same words at the exact same time, and you will be spiritually holding hands with people all around the world who wish you well. And so in closing, to old friends I say: I know you will be as pleased and excited about this book as I am. And to new friends . . . oh . . . what the heck, I'm going to say it anyway . . . Welcome to the Wonderful World of Daily Word!

Fannie Flagg is a successful actress, novelist, and screenwriter. Her books include *The New York Times* best-seller *Fried Green Tomatoes at the Whistle Stop Cafe*, *Daisy Fay and the Miracle Man*, and *Fannie Flagg's Original Whistle Stop Cafe Cookbook*. She received the prestigious Scripter's Award and was nominated for both the Writers Guild of America and an Academy Award for her screenplay of the movie *Fried Green Tomatoes*.

FOREWORD
BY BERNIE S. SIEGEL, M.D.

As a surgeon, I have seen numerous people who have had face-lifts, hoping that the operation would transform them. They would then appear younger and more attractive. However, many are disappointed with the results because surgery is only a temporary measure that cannot satisfy their real need to be loved and appreciated.

A true transformation can only happen at the soul level—a level much deeper than skin. What we truly need is a *faith*-lift, because faith is what transforms us; it is the real solution to all of life's problems.

The *Daily Word* magazine and this book help me by giving me that *faith*-lift and encouraging me to rely on my beliefs. Reading *Daily Word*'s messages keeps me in touch with myself, my feelings, and my life.

When we are encouraged and supported in that faith daily, we discover that every adversity becomes a catalyst for change. Just as charcoal under pressure becomes a diamond, we begin to understand that God doesn't punish us; God *redirects* us. No matter what is happening to us, our faith allows us to see God as our instructor and guide. Our faith in and love for God allow us to know the pure joy of living.

We have difficulties, and therefore many people see life as unfair. I don't think life is unfair, but it *is* difficult. A message that increases our spiritual awareness helps us deal with life's challenges and difficulties. The messages contained in this *Daily Word* collection act as a service manual for the soul. As we read it every morning or evening, it will inspire us to live the precious life we have been given to live. It is truly a traveler's guide to life.

I am reminded of how important each moment is when I jog through some of the old cemeteries here in New England. I love to read the headstones—they give me an idea of what people thought of life. It impresses me when a headstone leaves a precise message of a person's life: "Lived twenty-seven years, four months, and three days." How valuable and respected that time was for that person!

As meaningful as life is, often the going does get rough, and we need new inspiration. One day, jogging through one of my favorite cemeteries after a big snowstorm, I was struggling to create a path because no one had preceded me through the deep snow. I left my own deep footprints so that the next day it was a lot easier to jog because I was stepping in my own footprints. As in life, a lot of things are easier when we follow the path of those who have preceded us through difficult times. They can be our guides and teachers.

Five days later, I came back and the snow had frozen. By stepping in my "foot-made" path—which was now rigid and stiff—I was in danger of breaking an ankle. I had to step out and create a new path. That is what happens when we confront a new challenge: We have to find new inspiration and forge a new trail.

All religions teach us about the path or the way and its difficulties and how to deal with them. But the beauty of it is that we don't have to wait for a disaster to happen before we discover the direction that faith gives us. Through *Daily Word* and this book, we can be in touch with what can make our daily lives healthier and happier. *Daily Word* inspires us. Inspiration leads to revelation, and with revelation comes our own transformation and our *faith*-lift.

Bernie S. Siegel, M.D., practiced general and pediatric surgery in New Haven, Connecticut, until he retired in 1989. Author of *Love, Medicine & Miracles*; *Peace, Love & Healing*; and *How to Live Between Office Visits*, Siegel is actively involved in humanizing medical care, and he shares his techniques through speaking engagements and workshops.

Introduction

Many people tell me that when they open *Daily Word* magazine and read the message of inspiration for the day, they feel as if they are being embraced by their best friend. They ask, "Who else but a friend could know just what I need to hear to be inspired, to discover the strength and faith I never before realized I had, to celebrate with me in my triumphs, and to comfort me when I feel hurt?"

This is the way I feel about *Daily Word*, too. It's been my best friend for almost 30 years. We have grown up together, and I believe the peace of mind I enjoy is due in part to spending time with *Daily Word*.

And now this book is able to give us even bigger embraces and more inspiration. So when you turn to the first message, the last message, or any message in between, allow yourself to feel the love, inspiration, and prayer support that are there for you. Let the words increase your awareness of your own spirituality and goodness.

Any of the messages will speak to your heart, but if you are in the midst of a challenge or in need of inspiration, you may want to look in the index to find where relevant messages are located.

This book is a treasure chest of 365 invitations to the love, peace, health, and prosperity that we all deserve. And like a true friend, it will bring out the best in you.

One with you in prayer,
Colleen Zuck
Editor, *Daily Word*

Day 1

---◆---

I joyfully declare my oneness in spirit with all humankind.

ONE IN SPIRIT

Today, this very moment, is the perfect time to renew my sense of oneness with all humankind. I begin by closing my eyes and seeing neighbor helping neighbor in times of need. I envision children laughing and playing together in perfect harmony. I picture caring people from every nation holding hands, encircling the earth. I see each person allowing God to speak through him or her so that love and compassion reign.

I give thanks for the opportunity to be a loving brother or sister to those closest to me as well as to those in the farthest reaches of the world. I know there is no separation between us, no barrier or boundary that the love of God cannot overcome.

Renewed in spirit and filled with thoughts of love, I declare my oneness in spirit with all humankind.

"All the heavenly beings shouted for joy."
—Job 38:7

Day 2

I have time to spare and time to share.

A TIME AND SEASON

Most days, time is something that may seem in short supply. However, as the writer of Ecclesiastes so beautifully reminds everyone, "For everything there is a season, and a time for every matter under heaven."

So whatever is before me to accomplish this day, I will remember that I have time enough to do it with ease and efficiency. As I let go of my concern about due dates and quotas, I focus on what is before me to do. My time is used efficiently. I may even finish my projects with time to spare.

Today and every day I have time to spare and time to share. I share my time with others when they need a helping hand, and I share my time with God when I pray and meditate.

In every situation, I have all the time I need to accomplish my tasks successfully.

"It is time to seek the Lord."
—Hosea 10:12

Day 3

---◆---

God is gentle with me. I am gentle with myself.

GENTLE

I am in awe of God's power; however, it is God's gentleness that moves me.

God's will for me is that which is best for me; yet God does not force anything upon me. Patiently, God waits for me to be still, to turn within and listen.

God's gentle spirit is my foundation. When the cares of the world seem to overwhelm me and when challenges cause me to forget the truths that support me, God's spirit gently caresses me, uplifting and sustaining me.

Because God is gentle with me, I am gentle with myself and others. I do not condemn or speak hurtful words to others. My actions are ones that encourage the unfoldment of God's divine plan in myself and others.

Through gentleness and love, God's work is done.

"The fruit of the Spirit is love, joy, peace, patience, kindness, generosity, faithfulness, gentleness."
—Galatians 5:22–23

Day 4

—◆—

I receive power from God in the
silence of prayer.

SILENCE

There is magnificent power in quietness. For instance, the water erupting from the gates of a dam may capture my attention, but this great outflow is propelled forward by the power within the quiet, deep water behind the dam.

There is magnificent power in silence. In these quiet times of prayer, I turn my attention away from the confusion around me and attune myself to God.

In silence, I receive divine ideas for establishing new goals and new insights to overcoming familiar challenges.

A few moments in quiet prayer can be all that I need for my day to be transformed from one of disorder to one of divine order. In the silence, I open the floodgates of my soul and I am empowered by God for triumphant living.

"For God alone my soul waits in silence."
—Psalm 62:1

Day 5

—◆—

*I am creative, for God has given me talents
and abilities.*

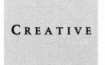

CREATIVE

I can accomplish great things, for
God has given me special talents and
abilities. However I choose to express
my creativity, I have confidence that I
will succeed.

Just as I can use my creativity to make a material
object, so can I create a positive, spirit-filled climate
around me. By focusing my thoughts on my ability to
communicate effectively with others, I help create a
friendly, harmonious environment.

I do not compare my talents to those of others,
considering others to be more talented than I am. I am
talented in my own way, just as others are talented in
their own ways. God gives each of us talents and
abilities, and I use mine creatively.

> "They are like trees planted by streams of water,
> which yield their fruit in its season,
> and their leaves do not wither."
> —Psalm 1:3

Day 6

—◆—

I contribute to and receive from a rich and abundant environment.

ENVIRONMENT Do I think of the environment in which I live as something apart from me or even foreign to me at times? Nothing could be further from the truth. I am part of an environment created by God.

Lovingly and thoughtfully, I contribute to the environment by living and working in accord with the people, animals, plants, and earth that make up the environment.

I may especially appreciate fresh air, clean water, lush vegetation, grand mountains, or sprawling plains that enrich my life. Being a good caretaker, I am responsible for maintaining such beauty and wonder.

I value the people who make up the environment of my home, my neighborhood, my workplace, and my whole world. I am both a giver and a receiver in a rich and abundant environment.

> "Think of us in this way, as servants . . .
> and stewards of God's mysteries."
> —1 Corinthians 4:1

Day 7

—◆—

*In prayer, I affirm that my loved ones
are being blessed.*

**PRAY FOR
OTHERS**

Loved ones can seem to have such serious needs that I may wonder if their needs can be resolved. How then do I pray? I pray with them and for them, affirming that they are being blessed:

"God, I pray for my loved ones and affirm that they are being blessed. I do not know what is best for them, but I know that You do. You are everywhere present. Therefore, Your healing, guiding, prospering presence is with my loved ones.

"You are with and within my loved ones right now. Your life sets into motion healing of mind, body, and emotions. You guide and prosper them in ways far and above the very best I can imagine. I give thanks that You are healing and guiding my loved ones right now."

**"If two of you agree on earth about anything you ask,
it will be done for you by my Father in heaven."**
—Matthew 18:19

Day 8

—◆—

As a creation of God, I am enriched with
potential and possibility.

POSSIBILITY

Perhaps I feel that in some relationship, job, or situation, I am capable of
giving more and being more.

I accept this feeling as something
positive—an inner urging to claim and experience the
great untapped potential that is within me. I can do
more and be more. I do not have to settle for less, for
as a creation of God, I am always in the process of
becoming more.

Each day I am moving forward to become something
greater than I have ever been in the past. No matter
what my age, I am never finished growing. My development is real and ongoing—moment to moment, day
to day, year to year.

I am a creation of God, and God has created me as
one who is enriched with potential and possibility.

"My Father is still working, and I also am working."
—John 5:17

Day 9

God will always stand by me.

STAND BY ME

God, I am Your beloved child, so I know that You will never forsake me. You will stand by me even if others have turned their backs on me. You love me unconditionally. You know what I have gone through and assure me that I did the best I knew how to do at the time.

You know my deepest thoughts and desires, and You love me. You are always ready to listen to me and guide me. At times I have been too distracted to listen, to even know that You are there with me, but You have never left me nor given up on me.

I am Your child—a creation of life and love. You let me know that there is no one else exactly like me. You love me with a love that knows no bounds. In a gentle whisper of assurance, You tell me that You will always stand by me.

"The Lord will not forsake his people."
—Psalm 94:14

Day 10

—◆—

I look at life with spiritual vision.

SPIRITUAL VISION

There is a way that I can meet unjust and inharmonious situations and maintain a peace-filled, faith-filled state of mind and heart. The way is to look at life with spiritual vision.

Spiritual vision allows me to see beyond the surface of matters and know what is true and enduring. Spiritual vision penetrates to the heart of every person and situation, calling forth divine possibilities.

I look at life with spiritual vision—an understanding and insight that radiates from God's spirit within me.

God's law of love and equity is working mightily in me, for me, and through me to bring forth blessings. God adjusts and corrects whatever needs a touch of the divine.

> "The Lord is my helper; I will not be afraid.
> What can anyone do to me?"
> —Hebrews 13:6

Day 11

—◆—

The love of God enfolds me.

LOVE God loves me in this very moment, just as I am. I do not have to change myself or perform some special task in order to earn divine love, for as God's child, I am loved freely and completely.

God's love for me is always present regardless of circumstances. Therefore, my actions in the past cannot deprive me of God's love. Through God's infinite love for me, I am continually nourished and encouraged to do better. The past is over, and God upholds me in doing my best right now.

God's love surrounds and enfolds me, uplifting me at all times. I am one with God's love, and it flows through me like a cleansing stream, healing past hurts and carrying me forward with great confidence.

Enfolded in God's love, I am at peace.

"God's love has been poured into our hearts through the Holy Spirit that has been given to us."
—Romans 5:5

Day 12

—◆—

In the garden of prayer, God enriches my soul with new understanding.

GARDEN OF PRAYER

By taking a nature walk, I may distance myself from the stress of work and everyday human affairs. In a secluded environment of peace and beauty, I look and listen with an enhanced appreciation for all I see and hear.

Taking a spiritual walk in my own inner garden of prayer can be even more helpful, for it enables me to hear and realize the Word of God as the very spiritual guidance I need.

Divine ideas flourish in my inner garden, waiting to be harvested by me. I attract the ideas that will bring positive and practical results through my faithful application.

No matter how busy I am, I can always take time to enter the garden of prayer. It is there I claim my divine inheritance and gather the fruits of Spirit.

> "Teach me the way I should go,
> for to you I lift up my soul."
> —Psalm 143:8

Day 13

—◆—

*My relationships are built on the
foundation of God's love.*

**FOUNDATION
OF LOVE**
God is love. As I allow God's love to
be the guiding force in my life, I lay a
firm foundation on which I build
happy, fulfilling relationships.

With God's love supporting and sustaining me,
harmonious relationships become the cornerstone for
greater expression of love in my life.

I have peace of mind, for I know that God's love
enfolds me and my loved ones when we are together
and when we are apart. At all times, God loves us.

Grounded on the firm foundation of God's love, I
know that I am loving. I am calm and serene as I talk
and interact with others. In the presence of God's love,
all my relationships are blessed and they bless me.

The more I put God's loving truths into practice in
my life, the stronger my foundation of love is.

**"God's firm foundation stands."
—2 Timothy 2:19**

Day 14

—◆—

I am immersed in the healing,
purifying light of God.

HEALING ENERGY

As I close my eyes, I begin to visualize myself aglow with life. God's healing energy is in every atom and cell of my body. I am immersed in healing, purifying light.

If there is an area of special need, I focus my attention on it and know that God's healing energy is doing its special work there.

I let go of any concern and trust the divine activity within that heals me and keeps me well and whole. I relax and let God's healing light renew me in mind and body.

God guides me on the path of health and healing, and I visualize this same healing energy working within my loved ones. No matter what the need, God's healing energy is greater.

In God's loving care, I am charged with new life.

> **"Then your light shall break forth like the dawn,**
> **and your healing shall spring up quickly."**
> **—Isaiah 58:8**

Day 15

—◆—

God blesses this new day!

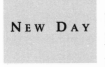

NEW DAY

Each morning, the sun rises on a beautiful new day, a day filled with hope. As I awaken, I give thanks and praise through prayer for a time of new opportunities.

Today I consider my thoughts and release those that may be unproductive or that fail to come from a spiritual awareness. Whatsoever things are good, whatsoever things are true—these are the thoughts I hold to this and every day.

I consider my words and speak only positive, constructive ones—words that praise and give thanks, words that speak of love and joy and understanding.

I consider my actions. I use each hour of the day in a positive, constructive manner. I make use of my God-given talents in affirmative and creative ways.

"Thank You, God, for this wonderful day!"

"This is the day that the Lord has made."
—Psalm 118:24

Day 16

—◆—

God is a real and loving presence within me.

LOVING PRESENCE — At times I may feel that the only way to avoid being lonely is to be with other people. Yet I might become disappointed when people do not provide me with the happiness I seek. I may then feel more alone than ever.

The truth is that I am never alone. My union with God is indivisible and undeniable. There is simply nowhere in the universe where God is not present. If I begin to feel alone, all I need to do is turn my attention to the loving presence of God within and around me.

Spiritually awakened, I realize that God has been with me all along, loving and patient, supportive and caring. I am never alone. The presence of God is a limitless resource of blessings that I can draw upon at any time, for any purpose.

> "You will make me full of
> gladness with your presence."
> —Acts 2:28

Day 17

—◆—

I am a spiritual being, vibrant and alive.

ZEST FOR LIVING
My vibrant zest for living has more to do with my attitude, outlook, and approach to life than the number of years that I have lived.

I do not associate my age or experience with my worth or abilities—whether I am too young or too old. Instead, I focus my attention on being a living expression of the eternal life and spirit of God. I am a spiritual being—wise, vibrant, and radiant.

Keenness of mind is a blessing for all who keep attuned to the spirit of God. I stay attuned to God in thought and prayer. By being receptive to God, I keep a fresh, positive outlook on life.

I am filled with a sense of the newness of life that is increasingly more evident through the power of God's spirit within me.

I am vibrantly and creatively alive!

"Take hold of the life that really is life."
—1 Timothy 6:19

Day 18

——◆——

In silence with God, I receive the gifts of peace, guidance, and healing.

GOD'S GIFTS

I gently close the door to all outer distractions and meet with God in the silence of my being. In the silence, I have a renewed awareness of God and God's gifts for me.

In silence, I receive the gift of peace and accept it into my life now. Peace is the cup I hold forth to be filled with all the blessings I am prepared to receive.

In silence, I receive the gift of guidance. It fills me, surrounds me, and lights my way. I go forth, living and walking in God's wonderful revealing light.

In silence, I receive the gift of healing. Healing springs forth from deep within me now. I am whole, well, and strong.

In silence, I claim God's gifts to me and say, "Thank You, God, for peace, guidance, and healing."

**"But whenever you pray, go into your room and shut the door and pray to your Father who is in secret."
—Matthew 6:6**

Day 19

—◆—

Through my unwavering belief in God, I am filled with faith and joy.

MY BELIEF IN GOD

My heart is filled with a joy that comes from knowing that I am a beloved child of God. Because I believe in the inexhaustible power of God, I live a happy, joy-filled life. I am continually blessed every minute of every day.

I believe that I am more than just a physical body. I am a spiritual being, filled with divine ideas. I know that if I believe that I am capable of doing something, I can do it!

I am able to face any situation with confidence, for Jesus promised, "All things can be done for the one who believes." Whatever my needs might be—health, prosperity, employment—God is guiding me to the fulfillment of these and all other needs. What a wonderful feeling it is to know that God is always here for me!

Daily I affirm: *Through my unwavering belief in God, I am filled with faith and joy.*

"Lord, I believe."
—John 9:38

Day 20

—◆—

I am well and healthy; I am strong and whole.

I Am

I AM is a powerful affirmation, for it proclaims the truth of my spiritual identity, which is the spirit of God within. I speak the words *I AM*, knowing that they bless whatever I connect them with.

I AM statements are founded on divine principle. When I affirm: *I am well and healthy; I am strong and whole,* I am declaring the truth about me—that I was created to live a life of health and well-being, strength and wholeness.

Because the cells of my body contain divine life and intelligence, they respond to powerful, life-affirming thoughts and statements.

The words *I AM* unite me in thought, word, and action with the health, prosperity, and understanding of God.

> "God said to Moses, 'I AM WHO I AM.'
> He said further, 'Thus you shall say to the Israelites,
> "I AM has sent me to you." ' "
> —Exodus 3:14

Day 21

—◆—

*I am a new person through
the indwelling spirit of God.*

**NEW
PERSON**
Perhaps I have been labeled "clumsy,"
"forgetful," or "shy" by others. Labels
have a tendency to stick—even over
many years. So what is the best way to
rid myself of such a label, to begin to believe in my own
self-worth?

I start being the new person I desire to be by declaring
that *I am* a new person through the indwelling spirit of
God. Now I begin to live my life in this manner. I am a
new person each day, for God within me is all the
intelligence, confidence, and poise I could ever need.

I know that I don't own any negative labels and
negative labels don't own me. Because I know that I am
a new person through God's spirit within, I will bring
divine qualities to all that I do.

> "You have stripped off the old self with its
> practices and have clothed yourselves with the
> new self, which is being renewed in knowledge
> according to the image of its creator."
> —Colossians 3:9–10

Day 22

—◆—

I live in God's eternal now.

ETERNAL NOW

In this, the present moment, I live, breathe, and have my being in God. Life takes on new meaning for me when I realize that each present moment is a part of God's eternal now.

When I live in the present, I have no regrets about the past. I bless the past but have no desire to relive it by recalling what happened in it. All that has gone before has brought me to the present moment.

My thoughts and attitudes in the now help prepare me for a positive future. My ability to deal with what is ahead of me is determined by how I use today's opportunities. Doors that seemed closed to me in the past may open today. New opportunities to love, forgive, and understand are eternally mine in the now moment with God.

"The Lord is a stronghold . . . in times of trouble."
—Psalm 9:9

Day 23

——◆——

I uplift my thoughts with spiritual vision.

UPLIFTED VIEW

The full joy of hiking may not be realized until I climb high enough up the mountain to see the far-reaching view of my world.

And raising my thoughts with spiritual vision is even more revealing, for it enables me to see a more inclusive view of all the blessings that are around me. I gain a greater awareness of myself and my relationship with God.

From this higher viewpoint, I see the whole picture, which is the true picture. Problems seem smaller and easier to handle and people appear closer to each other and more harmonious.

With a broader outlook, I realize that any new undertaking will involve changes in my present routine and thinking. Yet I know that such changes open the way for great possibilities in my life.

> "The path of the righteous is like the light of dawn,
> which shines brighter and brighter until full day."
> —Proverbs 4:18

Day 24

—◆—

I bless all God's children in my prayers.

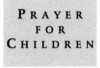

PRAYER FOR CHILDREN Today, as I think about children of every nation, I enfold them in my thoughts and prayers of love and faith. What is so meaningful about praying for children is knowing that they are receptive and responsive to positive, life-affirming prayers.

I give thanks that God's spirit is within each child. How gratifying it is to remember that although each child is unique, God expresses through all children as life, joy, intelligence, wholeness, and so much more.

Every time I pray for children, I see them filled with confidence, surrounded by peace, and inspired by the love of the adults around them.

I bless children in prayer, knowing that they bless me and others through their love, enthusiasm, and joy for living.

> **"Let the little children come to me . . . for it is to such as these that the kingdom of heaven belongs."**
> **—Matthew 19:14**

Day 25

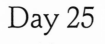

I concentrate on divine inspiration and I succeed.

CONCEN- TRATE

I find great satisfaction in doing my best. If the task before me is interesting or challenging, I give it my undivided attention without much effort. Then I am able to accomplish what I set out to do.

When activities seem boring or too complex, I may lose concentration and become distracted. Perhaps I put things off or leave tasks uncompleted. When this happens, I remind myself that God's all-wise, all-accomplishing spirit is within me, helping me establish my life in divine order.

Such concentration draws together scattered thoughts so that they are all in focus. My mental energies are brought to bear on the one subject or project before me.

Concentrating on the inspiration I receive from God assures me of success.

> **"Know well the condition of your flocks,
> and give attention to your herds."**
> —Proverbs 27:23

Day 26

—◆—

Wherever I am, the loving arms of God enfold me.

**S A F E
T R A V E L**

Before I begin a journey, whether I am vacationing abroad or visiting a nearby friend, I silently take a moment to affirm: *Dear God, I know that my way is made clear and that You will see me safely through this journey.*

Whatever my destination, I know that I am safe and secure in the loving arms of God. Because God's presence is continually protecting me, I am filled with trust and confidence and know that I will reach my intended destination. God's love surrounds me and fills me with a sense of peace. I am secure in the knowledge that God is with me wherever I go.

When I do reach my destination, I take a few moments to give thanks to God for protecting and guiding me along my path: "Thank You, God, for Your loving presence."

**"The Lord your God is with you wherever you go."
—Joshua 1:9**

Day 27

---◆---

I am an expression of God in my world.

DIVINE EXPRESSION

When I think about who I am, do I most often think of my human personality and characteristics? True, they are a part of me, but there is something much greater in me.

I am a spiritual being, for God's spirit is within me. When I truly see myself as an expression of God in my world, I will allow my divine nature to shine forth with brilliance in everything I do.

Because I am in tune with God, I draw on inner resources and know true fulfillment in whatever I do. All things *do* work together to bring about what is best for me and for everyone around me.

I am an expression of God in my world. As an expression of God in the world, I can lead the way to a new day filled with wonderful blessings.

> " 'In him we live and move and have our being';
> as even some of your own poets have said,
> 'For we too are his offspring.' "
> —Acts 17:28

Day 28

—◆—

I celebrate life in God's wonder-filled world.

CELEBRATE LIFE! I may be responding to the invitation written on the winds that is coming from backyard, countryside, lake, and mountain to look, listen, and explore. Through my senses, I take in the beauty and wonder of God's creation.

I may find myself in both familiar and unfamiliar surroundings celebrating life in the outdoors. I begin using muscles and energy I had forgotten I had.

As I celebrate life, I remember to bless my body, my activities, my journey with prayer. As I do, I prepare the way for happy, healthy, fulfilling activities and experiences.

I bless family and friends in prayer also. Whether I am with them or apart from them, God's spirit unites us in a celebration of life.

I enjoy both the busy and the relaxing times of each and every day.

"One who trusts in the Lord is secure."
—Proverbs 29:25

Day 29

—◆—

The life of God illumines and enlivens my body.

BODY TEMPLE

The very life of God pulses through me, cleansing, renewing, and rebuilding me.

My body is a temple of God, for the presence and power of God dwell within it. As keeper of that temple, I eat nourishing food, get needed rest, and replenish the liquids that maintain a life-giving flow during all activity.

I praise the adaptability and responsiveness that allow my body to adjust quickly to changing circumstances, time zones, and climates. The life of God illumines and enlivens my body.

I am grateful for my body's ability and agility. I have a reserve of strength when extra effort is needed. As one of God's beloved creations, I express health, wholeness, joy, and vitality.

> "If then your whole body is full of light . . .
> it will be as full of light as when a lamp gives
> you light with its rays."
> —Luke 11:36

Day 30

—◆—

I go within where God's peace,
wisdom, and love abide.

GOD ABIDES

If ever I feel that concerns are about to overwhelm me, I know that there is a place where I can find serenity and renewed faith. Right where I am, God is. Right where I am, peace and security abide.

I take a few deep breaths and concentrate on the presence of God that fills, uplifts, and heals me. I am blessed by a greater awareness of a loving and protecting Presence awaiting my recognition.

To go within, I open the door to the place where peace abides, wisdom guides, and love provides.

United with God, every day, every moment takes care of itself. My spirit, mind, and body settle into a harmonious whole. Oneness with the Creator is my reality.

> "Whenever you pray, go into your room and shut the door and pray to your Father who is in secret; and your Father who sees in secret will reward you."
> —Matthew 6:6

Day 31

—◆—

*God goes with me and gently guides me through
every experience.*

**GOD IN
CHARGE**
Does it seem that I have no control
over some of the situations in my life?
I remain calm, for I know that I don't
need to be in control because God is
in charge.

God is with me wherever I go and gently guides me.
In every situation, there is a right and fair outcome for
all concerned. I affirm this truth no matter what the
appearances may be.

I have faith that God is bringing together and including
me in a divine plan. Looking at my experiences with
faith helps me to recognize and act on the right guidance.
As I affirm that God is everywhere present, I accept the
blessings that are everywhere present and give thanks
for them. Because my words and actions are God-
directed, they help create an atmosphere of harmony
and love.

"Those of steadfast mind you keep in peace—
in peace because they trust in you."
—Isaiah 26:3

—————————— 31 ——————————

Day 32

—◆—

*My heart is filled with the love
of God.*

**HEART
BLESSING**
Today and every day, I bless my heart as I give thanks for the wonderful work that it does.

I focus my thoughts on the power and efficiency of my heart. Continuing to beat in perfect rhythm, my heart supplies my body with the nourishment and oxygen it needs.

The heart is a symbol of love, and rightly so, for divine love flows in and through my heart and radiates throughout my body. The love of God strengthens my heart, and I feel unburdened and free of doubt, worry, or fear.

I bless my heart and know that it constantly beats with faith and love, carrying life and energy to every cell of my body. Tension and stress are released, and I relax so that my heart can continue to function at its full capability.

"Wait for the Lord; be strong,
and let your heart take courage."
—Psalm 27:14

Day 33

—◆—

Because God is my guide,
I accomplish great things.

BREAK-THROUGH

What is the secret to any achievement? Is it wanting something enough or deserving something more than another person? No, it is neither.

I experience a true breakthrough to achievement when I move past simple wanting and striving to a powerful belief that I can reach my goals.

I break through the barriers of negative thinking—thinking I can't do something or don't deserve something. I realize that with God as my guide and strength, I can accomplish great things.

Do I want to end some negative habit or begin a positive one? Then I can! I can because I believe in the power of God within me and I let this belief support me in all my activities.

> "Jesus said to them, 'Do you believe that
> I am able to do this? . . . According to your faith
> let it be done to you.' "
> —Matthew 9:28–29

Day 34

—◆—

*My memory is a storehouse of divine ideas
and inspiration.*

MEMORY

I am attuned to the wisdom of God; therefore, I am able to retain and recall information easily and effortlessly.

My memory acts as a channel through which illumination, inspiration, and God-given ideas can continue to grow and be expressed.

Even during the most stressful situations, I can use my memory to its fullest ability. I do not force myself to recall facts or figures, but rather I follow what the Psalmist tells me: "Be still, and know."

I calmly allow God's spirit within me to take over. I know that being patient and relaxed helps me recall the information that I need to recall.

God's spirit is always at work, and I do not worry or fret. Through God's spirit within me, I am blessed with the ability to remember and recall divine ideas.

"Be still, and know."
—Psalm 46:10

Day 35

—◆—

I am whole, well, and free through the loving presence of God in me.

WHOLE The constant healing energy of God moves in and through me. I am whole in mind, body, and spirit.

My mind is alert and responsive. I am focused on what I need to do in every situation, for my thoughts are clear and positive.

My body is healthy and filled with vitality. I can accomplish whatever tasks lie ahead of me during the day. I eat the right foods and do what I need to do to keep my body healthy.

I dedicate my whole self to God. My faith assures me that both my spiritual and physical needs are met and that I am constantly being cared for by my loving Creator.

My mind, body, and spirit unite to radiate love and appreciation to God. I am filled with joy and assurance!

"May the God of peace himself sanctify you entirely; and may your spirit and soul and body be kept sound."
—1 Thessalonians 5:23

Day 36

—◆—

*Immersed in God's presence, I am
refreshed and ready to begin anew.*

**NEW
BEGINNING**

Was yesterday less than I hoped it
would be? That is okay, for I am not
bound by the past. Each new day is a
clean slate for me to write on. I let go
of the past and begin anew.

I devote time each day to becoming still, to becoming
immersed in God's presence and love. This feeling
of oneness with God renews my mind. I am open
to good.

Each time I experience God, I am refreshed. Together,
God and I fill the day with joyous activity. God guides
me so that I am giving as well as receiving blessings in
all my interactions with others.

At the end of my day, I give thanks that God is with
me in all that I do. I rest, knowing that tomorrow is
another new beginning filled with glorious possibilities.

"The eye is the lamp of the body. So, if your eye is
healthy, your whole body will be full of light."
—Matthew 6:22

Day 37

—◆—

God bless the caregivers of our world with strength, courage, and love.

CAREGIVER Thank God there are people who provide for the care and well-being of others. And perhaps I know and am praying with caring people who give much-needed service and attention to me or my loved ones. All around the world, people—professionals, family, and friends—are helping hands.

Caring for others day after day requires that a person be responsible, compassionate, and, most important, loving. God is working through caregivers and providing them with the faith, assurance, and wisdom to meet all situations.

I extend my love and blessings to the caregivers I know and to the caregivers of the world by affirming this prayer: *God blesses all caregivers with the strength and courage needed to care for others.*

> "Then I heard the voice of the Lord saying,
> 'Whom shall I send, and who will go for us?'
> And I said, 'Here am I; send me!' "
> —Isaiah 6:8

Day 38

—◆—

*I behold the glory of God in
my surroundings.*

**GOD'S
WORLD**

It is amazing how much I can learn about myself when I take the time to appreciate my environment.

Whether I am in the country or in the city, the beauty and diversity of God's creativity surround me and fill me with awe and wonder. I am constantly learning and growing in whatever environment I find myself.

Just as an oak tree stands sure and tall in a high wind, I stand sure in my faith in God. Through my unfailing faith, I know that I can and will overcome any seemingly negative circumstance.

Only God can create something as perfect and unique as a mighty oak tree or as tiny and powerful as an ant. Yet I, too, am an intricate part of God's world, for I am created in God's own image.

> **"In his hand is the life of every living thing
> and the breath of every human being."**
> —Job 12:10

Day 39

—◆—

I am aware that God's presence is within me and all around me.

A W A R E

During times of prayer, I build a deepening awareness of God's presence within me. This awareness of God within me enhances my perception of God within others.

I notice a hopefulness in situations where I had thought there was none. I observe a sacredness in other people regardless of their personalities or moods.

Aware of beauty in my world, I stir up the joy of living within me. My imagination is stimulated so that I am motivated to set new goals.

Because I am sensitive to the feelings of others, I listen in love and hear the joy, concern, or loneliness that is beyond the words they speak. I rejoice with them in their joy, and I pray with them that their every need is met.

> "Look to him, and be radiant;
> so your faces shall never be ashamed."
> —Psalm 34:5

Day 40

—◆—

I greet life with enthusiasm.

ENTHUSIASM

Each day is a time of great possibilities. Many experiences are before me that will inspire me on my upward path of growth and discovery. Knowing this, I greet each day with enthusiasm.

An enthusiastic attitude is an energizing one. When I am enthusiastic, I tap into an inner wellspring of energy that promotes change in my body and in my life.

The positive power that is generated by enthusiasm improves my circulation and helps restore health to my body. It stirs up joy within me and calls it forth into expression.

Enthusiasm for life brings out the beauty that I was once unable to see. It opens my eyes to the beauty in everyone and everything. When I approach life with enthusiasm, I accomplish my goals with ease and efficiency.

> "I came that they may have life, and
> have it abundantly."
> —John 10:10

Day 41

—◆—

Praise God! I am ready for a miracle!
I expect a miracle!

MIRACLE
What is a miracle? Is it some good that is so out of the ordinary, so unexplainable that I feel it is surely an act of God? Of course, miracles are from God, but they are a provision of divine law that is in effect at all times and for all people.

Knowing this is true, I am ready for a miracle. I acknowledge that according to the divine plan, miracles are happening—for me and for my loved ones. I expect and accept that the healing, prosperity, understanding, or peace that I so desire for myself and others is happening.

I maintain my faith in God and expect a blessing. Ready for a miracle, I do not limit myself or what I receive. No matter what the need may be, I expect a miracle and I accept a miracle!

"Ask, and it will be given you; search, and you will find;
knock, and the door will be opened for you."
—Matthew 7:7

Day 42

—◆—

God's love radiates from me to
bless others.

DIVINE
LOVE

There is power in divine love, and no matter how much I love, there is still more love within me to give. In fact, the more divine love I share, the greater my capacity to love. Divine love expands to fill my heart and reach out to others.

Love for one is never diminished by love for someone else. Love increases with giving. Surely this is grace from God. The gift of God's love, so freely given, blesses and heals each person it touches.

As my spiritual awareness increases, my love takes on a divine nature that sees God in all creation. I begin to recognize the beauty in everyone and in life itself.

God's love radiates from me to bless others, and my ability to love and be loving grows and grows.

> **"Many waters cannot quench love,**
> **neither can floods drown it."**
> **—Song of Solomon 8:7**

Day 43

—◆—

I give thanks for life and for the opportunity to become all that I can be!

AGELESS
Regardless of my age, each day is an opportunity to be reborn to a life of happiness and love and to celebrate my growing awareness of truth.

Happy birthday to a new me! I do not have to wait for my actual birth date to celebrate life. My life is so full of blessings that every day I give thanks to God:

"God, thank You for divine life, which energizes me and restores me to wholeness as it moves through my entire body.

"Thank You for divine light, which shines on me and through me to those I care for. Your light shows me the way.

"Thank You for unlimited blessings in my life, order in my affairs, and peace in my heart. Thank You, God, for the opportunity to become all that I am capable of being!"

> "You will have joy and gladness, and many will rejoice at his birth, for he will be great in the sight of the Lord."
> —Luke 1:14–15

DAILY WORD

Day 44

—◆—

I find joy in living by giving from the spirit of God within.

GIVING

I know people who find joy in living by giving of themselves. They speak a heartening word or perform some gracious act that transforms the day for the one who receives it.

Such giving is divine in nature. I, too, can truly give of myself when I give from the sacredness of my being. Speaking words of truth and sharing my joy, I give encouragement to those who seem down. I speak sincere and meaningful words of appreciation for others. I affirm words of life and strength to those in need of healing.

I give expression to the spirit of God in thought, word, and action. As I give of my true self—from my divine nature within—I greatly enrich my life.

"Give, and it will be given to you.
A good measure, pressed down, shaken together,
running over, will be put into your lap; for the
measure you give will be the measure you get back."
—Luke 6:38

Day 45

Thank You, God, for healing me!

**THANK
YOU, GOD**

God, I give thanks that healing is taking place in my mind, body, and affairs.

I welcome every evidence of healing, but I can and do give thanks in advance of anything I may see or feel. Giving thanks beforehand relieves me of fear or concern that might interfere with the healing taking place. I relax and let it happen.

I give thanks that a healing can come in an instant. I know also that it can develop over a period of time, so my faith remains strong and unwavering.

And, God, thank You for healing my loved ones. Although I may not be with them at all times, I know that Your healing presence is.

Thank You, God, for healing me and my loved ones.

> "The woman . . . fell down before him,
> and told him the whole truth. He said to her,
> 'Daughter, your faith has made you well; go in
> peace, and be healed of your disease.' "
> —Mark 5:33–34

Day 46

—◆—

*Each day God provides me with a new
beginning, a fresh start.*

**FRESH
START**

Do I wish that I could right a wrong
or correct a mistake by having the
chance to do something over?

The truth is that every day can be a
new beginning, a fresh start. Each day God gives me the
opportunity of a new day that I can mold into something fulfilling. I have the time—a fresh 24 hours—and
the capability—a gift from God—to do all I need to do.

Every relationship is renewed as I contribute more
understanding, gentleness, and love. Even routine
responsibilities begin to hold my interest as I acknowledge that whatever I do, I do my best.

I make a fresh start emotionally, physically, and
spiritually as I declare and follow through on this truth:
God provides me with a new beginning each day.

"I will sprinkle clean water upon you. . . .
A new heart I will give you, and a new spirit
I will put within you."
—Ezekiel 36:25–26

Day 47

—◆—

I experience growth through exercising my
spiritual power and potential.

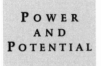

**POWER
AND
POTENTIAL**

Do I long to coast along in life for a while, to be free of responsibility?

By coasting, I might find temporary relief from seeming demands, but I must do more than coast to develop my full potential.

I choose to exercise my spiritual power and potential. Just as surely as exercising the physical body will develop muscles, so does exercising spiritual power develop the soul.

Any uphill journey can be one of spiritual progress and growth. I use spiritual power that enables me to become a better, wiser, healthier, more prosperous person than I was before.

I experience true growth through using spiritual power and potential.

"So neither the one who plants nor the one who waters is anything, but only God who gives the growth. The one who plants and the one who waters have a common purpose."
—1 Corinthians 3:7–8

Day 48

—◆—

The presence of God blesses my home with life, love, joy, and peace.

HOME BLESSING

Whether I live in a house or an apartment, in one room or many, I affirm that God is the one Presence and one Power within my home.

God is within me, within everyone who lives in my home, and within everyone who comes to visit. The presence of God permeates my home with life, love, joy, and peace.

Because the loving presence of God is in my home, a spirit of order and beauty shines in every room. My home is a haven of rest and contentment.

God is a loving counselor in family decisions, promoting understanding and cooperation.

The love of God fills my home, and all those who enter it are aware that they are in a haven of love and peace.

> "Choose this day whom you will serve . . .
> as for me and my household,
> we will serve the Lord."
> —Joshua 24:15

Day 49

—◆—

I am a center of divine love,
attracting and radiating blessings.

CENTER OF LOVE
I am a loving child of God. My soul grows in grace, beauty, and harmony as I rest in the awareness of God's love. Love radiates from me to family, friends, neighbors, and all people.

Love sees God's presence in every person and in every situation. It radiates forth to give without thought of receiving anything in return. Yet love is such a mighty force that it not only draws blessings to me, but also multiplies those blessings.

I am a radiating center of divine love. Only loving thoughts are welcome in my mind. Only words inspired by love pass my lips. All my actions are inspired by love.

Divine love fills me and overflows into all my activities. Divine love is the atmosphere in which I live, move, and have my being. Thank You, God!

"God lives in us, and his love is perfected in us."
—1 John 4:12

Day 50

—◆—

I express love and appreciation for those who have blessed and inspired me.

GUIDING LIGHTS   Throughout my life, I have been and continue to be influenced in powerfully positive ways by teachers, loving friends, and family.

Just as a lighthouse is a much-needed guide to a ship in a storm, these special people have helped guide my way. In celebration of these guiding lights, I take time today to give thanks to God for their love and inspiration.

As I travel down the path of life, it is comforting to know that I can learn from the experiences and observations of others. I am able to gain knowledge from the road that they have traveled before me.

Today I express my love and appreciation for the people who have blessed and inspired me. God has given me the wonderful gift of their positive presence in my life.

> **"I will bless you, and make your name great,
> so that you will be a blessing."
> —Genesis 12:2**

Day 51

—◆—

My mind and body are healed through the power of God's love.

HEALING   Physical pain or discomfort may draw my attention to a particular healing need. Immediately I begin to pray, affirming health and life and giving myself the care and attention I need.

I do all that I can to cooperate with God's healing love, knowing that even before the need arose, God lovingly provided for me.

Emotional pain can seem so real that it will eventually affect my physical well-being. So I seek healing of my thoughts and emotions just as I do for a physical challenge. I pray, believe the best, and cooperate with the healing that is mine through the power of God's love.

To maintain health of mind and body, I continue this positive, life-affirming pattern, declaring: *Thank You, God, for Your healing presence. My mind and body are restored through the power of Your love.*

"He had faith to be healed."
—Acts 14:9

Day 52

—◆—

*God is continually giving me
opportunities for new beginnings.*

**BEGIN
ANEW**
One of the important lessons in my
spiritual development is learning to
release the past so that I can live fully
in the now, in the presence of God.

I know that I bring my past with me to any new
beginning, but I choose to take only whatever adds to
my enrichment and upbuilding. I carry with me the
understanding I have gained from my experiences, but
I let go of the excess baggage of guilt and regret.

As I do, I gain greater knowledge from each new
experience. God is continually giving me new understanding and the opportunity of a new beginning.

I release myself and others from limitations from the
past and the mistakes in the past. I choose to let go of
yesterday's mistakes and begin anew.

**"For once you were darkness, but now in the
Lord you are light."
—Ephesians 5:8**

Day 53

—◆—

God's healing life fills me and
restores me. I am whole.

LIFE

God created me to express life, light, and total well-being. I know this is the truth about me even in the midst of a seeming challenge to my health.

I take action in doing whatever is necessary to maintain an awareness of health and wholeness. If I am receiving assistance in healing, I remind myself that God is with me and everyone assisting me.

God loves me wherever I am, guiding every decision and every move concerning my well-being.

The life of God fills every cell of my body. As I hold to thoughts of God's healing life, I allow my body to accept health as a true reality. I am secure, whole, and well.

If people dear to me are in need of healing, I affirm that God's healing life fills them through and through. They, too, express life and well-being.

"With you is the fountain of life."
—Psalm 36:9

Day 54

—◆—

As God's apprentice, I help create a bountiful world of blessings.

APPRENTICE There is no limit to God's creative ability. Created in God's image, I am fashioned to be creative, too.

God has provided the material for building homes and other structures, and has given humanity a rich earth and food supply so that all can be nourished. God instilled each person with love and compassion so that people are eager to help one another. God granted every person grace so that the world knows it is okay to make a mistake.

Through right use of what God has given me, I am God's apprentice. The tools I use are divine guidance, intuition, faith, and love. Whether I discover a better way to do something, form a new friendship, or work at redeeming a social condition, God is my instructor and guide. Together we create a bountiful world of good.

"For in him all things in heaven and on
earth were created."
—Colossians 1:16

Day 55

—◆—

I think thoughts and speak words of health and wholeness.

HEALTH AND WHOLENESS Only thoughts of health and wholeness linger in my mind, and only words expressing radiant health and strength are in my conversations.

I think about the things I love to do as a strong and healthy child of God. If I am not able to do these things at this time, I hold to a vision that moves me toward health and wholeness.

I build a vocabulary of healing words of life and sprinkle them through my conversations. I fill my mind with love, joy, and the renewing life of God. In the quiet of my own being, I let these ideas work.

Then, as I go about my daily activities, I expect to be healthy and strong. I rejoice and give thanks for the health I am expressing now.

"The centurion answered, 'Lord . . . only speak the word, and my servant will be healed.' "
—Matthew 8:8

Day 56

—◆—

Each day brings new discoveries and new adventures into my life!

DISCOVERIES I eagerly greet each new day with enthusiasm for the discoveries that are in store for me. New possibilities abound; I have only to claim them.

I make new discoveries by being open to enriching activities, such as attending classes on subjects or themes that interest me. Or I may simply take a different route to or from home.

I embark on new adventures in life by meeting new people. Every new face is an opportunity for friendship.

No matter how I decide to pursue new discoveries, I know that God is continually guiding me to right activities. God's presence is with me, and I am filled with joy and enthusiasm as I eagerly await each new adventure.

"Ask, and it will be given you; search, and you will find; knock, and the door will be opened for you."
—Matthew 7:7

Day 57

---◆---

Thank You, God, for taking such good care of me.

GOD CARES

God's spirit is within me; God's protecting presence goes with me wherever I go, enfolding me, guiding me, and nurturing me.

Even as I sleep, God's life and intelligence in the organs and systems of my body are doing the wondrous work of sustaining and nourishing me.

God's mighty healing activity constantly moves throughout my mind and body, restoring me to wholeness.

My mind is continually filled with radiant, divine ideas that brighten my life and fulfill me completely.

For all this and even more, I say: "Thank You, God, for loving me so! I return Your love to You and to all creation. Living and moving in a circle of divine love, I am taken care of and blessed in every way."

"Cast all your anxiety on him, for he cares for you."
—1 Peter 5:7

Day 58

—◆—

I thank God for my loved ones!

NURTURING LOVE I give thanks for the people who have loved and nurtured me, who have cared for and about me—in an immediate crisis or over a lifetime.

Through prayer and thanksgiving, I express appreciation to God for these special people. Whether I am blessed with treasured memories of dear ones or their continuing presence in my life, I am thankful that they helped me gain or renew my sense of security and self-worth.

Today I give thanks for these special people. I appreciate all that I am and all that I am becoming through the help and inspiration of the people who have loved me.

Regardless of age or circumstance, I realize that the joys of a loving relationship never diminish, but forever enrich me.

> "We must always give thanks to God for you,
> brothers and sisters beloved by the Lord."
> —2 Thessalonians 2:13

Day 59

—◆—

God is my strength, and I face each day filled with peace.

FEARLESS There may be times when I find myself in an unfamiliar place and feel concern or alarm. During these times I remember and affirm the Psalmist's assurance that God is "my rock and my salvation, my fortress; I shall never be shaken."

I remain calm in all situations because I know that God is with me. I acknowledge God's presence in my life, and I react accordingly throughout the day.

I am fearless and do not let my emotions control me. Through my faith in God's protecting presence, I face the day confident and free from concern.

Thank You, God, for Your protection and love. I choose to live fearlessly and take control of my life. I am not a prisoner of fear; rather, I am powerful in my faith.

**"God did not give us a spirit of cowardice, but rather a spirit of power and of love and of self-discipline."
—2 Timothy 1:7**

Day 60

—◆—

*In prayer, I am totally centered
in God.*

**GOD'S
CALL**

The call to prayer is sounded in my heart. I become still and relax. In prayer, I cease all striving and release personal desires and needs to God.

Every shadow is erased by God's light. Every problem is dissolved by divine wisdom. Every error is canceled by divine love. I rest in God's presence.

God's presence has sounded the call to prayer. As I turn to God, I am quickened with the confidence that I can be the person I truly want to be. I can accomplish the things I long to accomplish.

My mind is receptive to divine light; my heart, to divine love; my body, to divine life. My environment is filled with God's peace and harmony. My affairs are set in order by God's prospering power.

> **"You show me the path of life.
> In your presence there is fullness of joy."
> —Psalm 16:11**

Day 61

God gives me the ability to remember the good.

God has given me the ability to recall memories of loved ones, not so that I can live in the past, but so that I will be blessed and uplifted now.

Although these people may have passed on to another level of existence, I can remember their faces and the events that have special meaning for me. More important, I remember that our real connection is a spiritual one which is eternal.

If my memories of people and events are not fond ones, I can begin to forgive myself and others for words that may have been said or actions that may have taken place. As I release negative thoughts, new avenues for love, understanding, and harmony open before me.

My day is made brighter through my remembrances, but each day is a fresh opportunity to create new memories.

"I will not forget you."
—Isaiah 49:15

Day 62

I pray and give thanks for parents and for all people who have blessed me.

PARENTS

The role of a parent is one of great responsibility, yet it is also one of immense joy and rewards.

Today, I bless the special people who have played an important role in my life. I give thanks for those who have nurtured me, listened to my dreams, and gently guided me along my way.

I bless mothers and fathers everywhere. I bless grandparents, friends, and other loved ones whose support and love have encouraged others to be who they are—unique people of worth and importance. I bless teachers who have appeared when they were needed the most, sharing so many valuable lessons with their students.

I pray that all who fulfill the role of a parent will live up to God's standard by giving unconditional love.

"Honor your father and your mother."
—Exodus 20:12

Day 63

—◆—

*I am an expression of divine love,
wisdom, life, and abundance.*

**GOD'S
CREATION**
God created me to be an expression of divine love, and being that expression of divine love to my family and friends blesses me.

God created me to be an expression of divine intelligence. My thoughts are orderly. In divine cooperation, my actions reflect the wisdom of my thoughts.

God created me to be an expression of divine abundance. Knowing that all my blessings come from God, I share them willingly and generously with others.

God created me to be an expression of divine life. I understand that radiant life is perfection of mind and body, and I give full expression to life.

Knowing who I was created to be, I go forth today fulfilled by and giving expression to the love, wisdom, life, and abundance of God.

> **"Be perfect, therefore, as your heavenly
> Father is perfect."**
> —Matthew 5:48

Day 64

—◆—

God is my true friend and encourages me to be a friend to others.

DIVINE FRIEND I reflect on what a true friend God is to me. God is my most trusted companion, the One who always desires the best for me. God's friendship inspires me to pass the blessing of friendship on to others. My life can be the gospel of a true friend, the good news of friendship.

Wanting to be a friend to all, I ask God to guide me. Aware that friendship is more than kind words and casual agreement, I seek the courage, wisdom, and inner peace that are needed to be a friend in good times and in times of challenge.

As I think of the special people who contribute so much good to my life, I realize why God provided me with friends. True friends touch me at a deep level of love and understanding. My friendships remind me to love with the unconditional love that is the divine pattern for all.

"A friend loves at all times."
—Proverbs 17:17

Day 65

—◆—

I see God's light in all people and circumstances.

**LIGHT
TOUCH**

Throughout the day, no matter whom I meet or what situations may arise, I focus my attention on God's light within all people. I use this truth to give the light touch in all my interactions with them.

I see the light in others—God's light of love and wisdom. I possess this light, too, and it shines forth from me as a beacon of harmony and peace. By giving the light touch to everyone I meet, I radiate an optimistic attitude. My heart is filled to overflowing with unfailing love for and acceptance of all God's children.

My positive attitude is born of a wonderful knowledge—the knowledge that God's spirit is within me and within all others.

As I give life the light touch, my day is made brighter and my way is made easier. I am free from doubt or concern.

**"In the Lord you are light. Live as children of light."
—Ephesians 5:8**

Day 66

—◆—

God, who created me, is constantly renewing and restoring me.

WHOLENESS OF LIFE

God, the divine spirit that created me, is within me always. God's spirit is now renewing my mind. I think clearly, remembering what I need to remember and freely letting go of thoughts that would disturb me and my well-being.

God's spirit moves freely through every part of my body—renewing every function, joint, and fiber. I rejoice that the ever-renewing spirit of God is quietly at work within me even as I sleep.

God's spirit is now restoring my soul to its original, pristine beauty. This restoration is one of wholeness. I am renewed in spirit, soul, and body.

I am thankful that God, who created me, remains with me always and is continually restoring me. I am healthy and whole.

> **"He leads me beside still waters;**
> **he restores my soul."**
> **—Psalm 23:2-3**

Day 67

—◆—

I am filled with hope, for the presence and power of God are within me.

HOPE

In any situation, there is one Presence and Power that dispels fear and doubt. Knowing that the presence and power of God is within me instills me with hope. Because I have hope, I help prepare the way for miraculous things to happen.

Hope may be a gentle nudge that guides me in the direction I need to take. Whether the situation is one in which there is a need for healing, increased abundance, or harmony in a troubled relationship, hope lifts me above the outer appearance of things to the realization that "for God all things are possible."

Nothing can extinguish the presence and power of God that glow within me. Through positive prayer and affirmation, I support God's plan for great possibilities.

"We have this hope, a sure and steadfast anchor of the soul, a hope that enters the inner shrine behind the curtain."
—Hebrews 6:19

Day 68

---◆---

Through God's presence within, I am calm and serene.

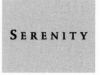

SERENITY

How can I convince myself to be calm no matter what is going on around me? The way to serenity does not come through convincing; it comes through God's presence within me.

Am I working toward overcoming some habit? I am never alone in my overcoming; God's presence within strengthens me and encourages me along the road to complete recovery. The will of God fulfills me.

If I am going to take a test, I affirm that the presence of God goes with me into the classroom or examination room. Before and during any test, I silently declare that the presence of God within me is healing life and guiding light.

Through the presence of God within, I am calm and serene.

"And he woke up and rebuked the wind and the raging
waves; they ceased, and there was a calm."
—Luke 8:24

Day 69

—◆—

*God's healing power moves through me now,
and I am healed.*

GOD'S HEALING POWER

No matter what form a healing challenge may take, there is power within that heals me. This healing power is God's spirit within me.

As I pray, I visualize God's healing life moving through me as a current flowing from the top of my head to the soles of my feet. I hold to a vision of healing despite any outer appearances to the contrary.

While I am praying, I include others in need of healing. I know the truth for them just as surely as I know it for myself. I see them completely healed in mind and body. I am thankful that God answers prayer.

No healing challenge is too great for God's power to dissolve. I trust completely that God is guiding me and my loved ones on paths of health and healing. I rejoice that God's healing power is moving through us right now.

**"Your faith has made you well."
—Matthew 9:22**

Day 70

—◆—

*Each moment is a precious, God-given
opportunity for me.*

**EACH
NEW
MOMENT**

Each moment is a fresh opportunity
from God to begin anew.

Because each moment is precious, I
do not allow outgrown attitudes and
behavior from the past to govern me. Past mistakes may
indicate the outlook that I held then, but the newness of
each moment allows greater unfoldment within my
spirit, mind, and body.

I am free to live life as fully as I can envision it. New
inspiration energizes me and leads me in new and
rewarding directions. With each new moment, I am free
to discover and make use of inner potential that I may
not have known existed.

As I live life in the present moment, I am prepared to
accept the joy that it contains. My activities take on
new meaning. Life becomes much smoother and easier
as I accept the flow of blessings coming to me now.

**"Beloved, we are God's children now."
—1 John 3:2**

Day 71

—◆—

With a firm faith in God,
I am confident of right outcomes.

STAND FIRM

If I feel that I have been unjustly treated, my first reaction might be to defend myself vigorously. Yet such an emotional reaction can often stir up both inner and outer turmoil that further complicates the situation.

Then how do I respond? I choose to express an attitude that will eliminate conflict and bitterness. Moses spoke so clearly of this attitude when he said, "Do not be afraid, stand firm, and see the deliverance that the Lord will accomplish for you today."

God's love and order work for me every day. Even when I am in the midst of what seems to be an unjust situation, I know divine love and order are working. My faith-filled attitude saves me from emotional upset and prepares me for right outcomes. I stand firm.

"Do not be afraid, stand firm, and see the deliverance that
the Lord will accomplish for you today."
—Exodus 14:13

Day 72

—◆—

Knowing I am one with God fulfills the longing of my heart.

ONE WITH GOD

There is a great longing in the heart of all humanity to know and feel the presence of God.

In truth, no person can ever be separated from God, but still some feel that a connection must be made; they long for a reunion. Often, people go to great effort trying to fill this longing in outer ways.

The answer lies in turning to God in prayer: "Dear God, Your love fills my heart, and I respond to that love now. My heart sings with joy, and I feel the warmth of Your Presence surrounding me softly, tenderly.

"You know my hopes, my dreams, and my needs. I turn them over to You, and listen so that I may know Your wonderful will for me. Each day as I pray, I am more aware of my oneness with You. What a great feeling this is! Thank You, God."

"The Lord is near to all who call on him."
—Psalm 145:18

Day 73

God leads me to and sustains me in right and fulfilling employment.

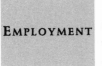

EMPLOYMENT

If I or a loved one is seeking employment, I remember that our welfare in this and all other matters is important to God. God knows our needs and will lead us to the places where we can use our abilities and discover new ones.

A trusting heart and a receptive mind inspire me with confidence and give me the inner assurance that I am endowed with wisdom, creativity, and strength.

If a new path is revealed to me, I am willing to try it. With a positive outlook and an expectant heart, I move forward to right and fulfilling employment.

Working conditions may change, but God is change-less and enduring. I hold fast to the truth that God is with me in all ways, guiding and directing me in the work I do and in new ways of expression.

"The Lord your God is with you wherever you go."
—Joshua 1:9

Day 74

—◆—

I am calm and confident, for God is always with me.

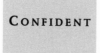

CONFIDENT

What a blessing it is to know that there is a power within me guiding me through the events of this day.

If discord develops between me and a loved one, co-worker, or even a stranger, I am poised. I know that harmonizing thoughts, words, and actions initiated by me and others can establish order.

I relax and center my thoughts on God's presence within me. As I concentrate on the presence of God, doubt is transformed into confidence.

Wherever I am, God is. God has given me a spirit of confidence and love. Whatever I need, God will provide. I gratefully receive prosperity, healing, guidance, and strength.

Whatever I seek, God will reveal to me. God's presence guides and uplifts me. I am calm and confident.

"Do not, therefore, abandon that confidence of yours; it brings a great reward."
—Hebrews 10:35

Day 75

—◆—

Each day I am unfolding into a more resilient and fulfilled person.

UNFOLDMENT God has given me the ability to think clearly and creatively and the freedom to be the pilot of my own life. Therefore, I can change my thoughts and habits to ones that more fully express the best about me.

I am free to discard any behaviors I no longer find rewarding. I can remove from my mind thoughts of doubt or guilt. I replace these thoughts with a confident realization that I can discern a better way. I rejoice that I continue to grow and unfold.

I do not have to be perfect, but I can make progress each day toward doing a little better than I did the day before. I have not failed as long as I keep trying. I gain such satisfaction and self-esteem with each accomplishment that I have the confidence to attempt new adventures.

"So neither the one who plants nor the one who waters is anything, but only God who gives the growth."
—1 Corinthians 3:7

Day 76

---◆---

God is the source of all blessings.
I expect and accept my blessings now!

EXPECTATIONS

To pray with expectancy is to pray with the assurance that I am participating in sacred communion with God.

I pray with this expectancy, knowing that all my needs will be met in the right time and in the right way. As Jesus assured me, "Whatever you ask for in prayer with faith, you will receive."

My expectation is grounded in my faith in God as the source of all blessings. I expect and know that I am receiving abundance in my life. My needs are being met.

I expect and accept that I was created to be healthy. My mind is alert and enthusiastic, and my body is strengthened and filled with energy. The life force of God flows through me, nourishing and revitalizing each cell.

God is the source of all blessings. I expect and accept my blessings now!

"Whatever you ask for in prayer with faith,
you will receive."
—Matthew 21:22

Day 77

*I am alive with the eternal life
of God.*

If I believe that my faculties will diminish and I will slow down as I add years to my life, I need to change my thinking. The truth is that I am made in the divine image, that I am alive with the eternal life of God.

My life may be divided into units of time which I call past, present, and future, but the foundation of my existence is in eternity. No matter what my age, I can remain youthful in outlook and spirit. I can continue to grow and learn and develop. I can be vitally alive, functioning efficiently throughout the years of my life.

I joyously affirm that I am not subject to limitation. I am a spiritual being now and always. I am flexible and adaptable. I am constantly growing in spiritual awareness, fashioning my life after the divine pattern.

"All of us . . . are being transformed into the same
image from one degree of glory to another."
—2 Corinthians 3:18

Day 78

—◆—

The life of God renews my mind and body.
I am well.

RENEWING LIFE

To be renewed is not just to be repaired or reconditioned; it is to be made new! I am made new through the life of God within every cell of my body.

I do not limit my health and well-being by thinking about symptoms or conditions. If I do experience pain or discomfort, I affirm the renewal of mind and body through the perfect life of God within me, which overcomes all. I am whole and well.

Although it can, renewal of my mind and body may not come in an instant. Each day I may notice that I feel better—stronger and more energetic—than I did the day before. As I acknowledge and give thanks for my healing, I contribute to the ongoing renewal process within me.

"Be renewed in the spirit of your minds, and . . . clothe yourselves with the new self, created according to the likeness of God in true righteousness and holiness."
—Ephesians 4:23–24

Day 79

—◆—

The love of God fills my heart with peace.

INNER PEACE

Do I see myself as limited in some way? I may think of myself as being less than I should be. However, I discover great inner peace when I understand that God sees me as I was created to be: perfect in every way, not defined by events or circumstances.

God loves me the way I am. Although I change and grow from day to day, I will always be loved just as much as I am this minute.

Since God's love for me is immeasurable, I need never feel lost or alone. Even in the darkest moments, God is with me. Turning my attention to God, I feel at peace in the presence of pure love.

God, my greatest supporter, has absolute faith in me even when I seem to have none. I soar to new heights of achievement on the wings of God's love.

"I have loved you with an everlasting love."
—Jeremiah 31:3

Day 80

—◆—

*God keeps me steady and secure through
every change.*

**STEADY
AND
SECURE**

The seasons of life unfold—all in
divine order. I know this is the truth
about me as well. I grow through
continuing cycles of change, yet I am
stable, steady, and secure through each one because I
keep in mind my oneness with God, the underlying
reality which remains the same forever.

God strengthens me when I feel weary. God inspires
me when circumstances seem bleak. During times of
rest, I am refreshed so that I can begin again, renewed in
spirit, soul, and body.

God keeps me steady so that I can be a radiating
center of life, light, love, order, and peace. I make a
positive contribution to my family, my co-workers, my
community, my country, and my world. I remain stable,
secure, and undisturbed by the winds of change.

"For I the Lord do not change. . . . Return to me,
and I will return to you."
—Malachi 3:6–7

Day 81

---◆---

*God's harmonizing spirit fills me and overflows
from me to others.*

HARMONY

Dear God, today I open my mind
and heart to Your loving, harmonizing
spirit. Fill me now to overflowing with
love. Let me be Your representative and
express Your love and harmony wherever I go.

I radiate a friendly spirit to others—a spirit of
gentleness, patience, and loving kindness. My words
are words of peace. In every situation, I see beyond
appearances to Your indwelling presence.

I have unlimited love to share with others. My
disposition is sweetened by Your spirit flowing through
me. My human relationships are harmonized and
transformed as Your love finds expression through me.
Peace, contentment, and happiness are mine.

Thank You, God, for making me a blessing as I
express Your harmony in my life.

> **"If we love one another, God lives in us,
> and his love is perfected in us."**
> **—1 John 4:12**

Day 82

---◆---

I am eternally young in spirit.

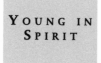

YOUNG IN SPIRIT

I am young in spirit because I am eternally one in spirit with God. I am interested in all the wonder that God created.

I am interested in the progressive unfoldment of this planet. I am interested in other people—the young and not so young—what they do and what they think.

I am young in spirit because I keep up with the times. I am open to new ideas and feel enthusiastic about new possibilities.

I am young in spirit because I maintain a joyous sense of humor and spontaneity. I smile readily, laugh heartily, and love to try my hand at something new.

I stay young in spirit because I eat wisely, exercise regularly, rest sufficiently, and pray daily. Above all, I remain young in spirit because I know that I am eternally alive in God.

> **"Your youth is renewed like the eagle's."**
> **—Psalm 103:5**

Day 83

*Centered in the presence of God within me,
I relax.*

RELAX

I always do myself and those around me a favor when I relax and release pressure and tension. Actually, relaxation is an attitude of mind as much as it is inactivity. When I carry with me a complete realization of the presence of God, my daily responsibilities do not exhaust me. I relax and enjoy what I am doing instead of allowing tension and anxiety to dissipate my creative energy.

The most effective way for me to continue to develop the state of mind that permits relaxed and peaceful living is through prayer. As I take time every day—even if only for five or ten minutes—to let my thoughts be on the presence of God within me, I will realize a sense of true peace. Relaxed and at peace, I gain a perspective on life that promotes my good and the good of others.

> "Those of steadfast mind you keep in peace—
> in peace because they trust in you."
> —Isaiah 26:3

Day 84

---◆---

I am divinely guided in keeping all lines of communication open.

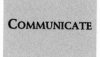

COMMUNICATE

I help to establish order in both personal and business relationships by keeping the lines of communication open. I can do this by projecting an air of friendliness and objectivity to my friends and co-workers. In this way, I know that the things that need to be brought out into the open will be discussed in a calm and rational manner.

Communication is also listening to what others have to say. I am open to their ideas, for I know that God speaks to and through all who are willing to listen and communicate.

Open communication with others encourages me to become more relaxed and in harmony with those around me. I am divinely guided to keeping all lines of communication open, and I am receptive to what others have to say.

"The sheep hear his voice. He calls his own sheep by name and leads them out."
—John 10:3

Day 85

—◆—

Divine love instills wisdom within me. I follow a divinely directed path.

GUIDANCE No decision is too difficult to make when I realize that I have the wisdom of God within me. There is no misunderstanding that cannot be resolved when I allow the love of God to guide me.

In the silence of prayer, I become still and realize that the love of God is flowing throughout my being. I recognize divine love as the one true source of all the guidance I will ever need. I know that as divine order works through me, it will bring harmony to every circumstance of my life.

I give thanks to God for divine guidance, and I am grateful that it is available to me at all times. Wisdom and good judgment are mine when I follow the guidance I receive. I know that I am being divinely directed to the path that will lead me to my greatest happiness and success.

"With all wisdom and insight he has made known to us the mystery of his will."
—Ephesians 1:8–9

Day 86

—◆—

This is a divine appointment day—a day of discovery and sharing blessings.

DIVINE APPOINTMENT

The most routine task or the most complex situation can be a divine appointment for me. Every opportunity in which I express the qualities God has given me is one that leads to greater well-being.

A chance meeting with someone may establish a mutually supportive and meaningful friendship. So I greet each person as a potential friend.

My skills and experiences can pave the way for a divine appointment with someone I can help through a particularly challenging time.

Taking a new course of action or a new class may be the beginning of a more prosperous and fulfilling job opportunity.

When I know that every day is a divine appointment day, I am eager to discover new blessings and to share my blessings with others.

"I am longing to see you so that I may share with you some spiritual gift."
—Romans 1:11

Day 87

---◆---

Trusting God, I am free to do my finest and best.

FREEDOM

I release any unpleasantness from the past and let it sail away. I envision it going through the mists of my memories, over the horizon, and out of sight.

Love rushes in to fill any empty places within my heart or mind. Now I am free to do what is before me and free to do it better than ever before. I am free to enrich my life and everything concerning me.

In releasing the past and doing my very best today, I am free with the freedom of Spirit. I do not worry about tomorrow. A well-lived today is the cornerstone on which a greater tomorrow stands.

As I trust God to prepare the way before me, I am free to do my finest work and to make my greatest strides in soul growth.

"In returning and rest you shall be saved;
in quietness and in trust shall be your strength."
—Isaiah 30:15

Day 88

—◆—

I live in the now, giving thanks for the blessings each day contains.

TODAY Trying to relive the past or predict what is to happen in the future can keep me from enjoying the present moment. Therefore, I make a commitment to live in the *now*, secure in the knowledge that God is in charge and all is well.

If I ever find myself feeling overwhelmed by the complexities of life, I remember that I can live only one day at a time. I know I have the faith, strength, and courage to turn any challenge into an opportunity for spiritual growth.

I do not allow memories to stand in the way of today's blessings. I let go of the past and open the door to new blessings. I do my best and leave the rest to God.

I think thoughts that are positive and uplifting. Such thoughts fill my day with joy and act as a magnet that draws amazing experiences to me.

"Now is the acceptable time."
—2 Corinthians 6:2

Day 89

—◆—

The spirit of God calms my mind.
I radiate peace.

RADIATE PEACE   How can I manage to live in a busy world and still remain calm? I can do so through prayer—by centering myself in the peace of God.

Daily communion with God keeps me grounded in peace. Through prayer, I make conscious contact with the peace of God within me. I then not only feel at peace, but I also radiate peace.

The best way to remain centered in the peace of God is to set aside time each day for spiritual communion with God. Prayer and meditation take my awareness back to God, the source of peace. While resting in the silence, I am immersed in God's love. My thoughts are calmed. Centered in the peace of God, I see my way clearly. I come away from this time refreshed and renewed.

"Incline your ear, and come to me;
listen, that you may live."
—Isaiah 55:3

Day 90

—◆—

I rejoice in a celebration of life!

REJOICE   What reason do I need to celebrate life? A birthday, a wedding anniversary, or a holiday are all reminders that there is something to celebrate.

Yet every day can be a celebration of life. I celebrate life by praising God. Praise can be a quiet time of communion with God or a joyous hymn of thanksgiving to God.

I celebrate by recognizing the life of God within others. We are all unique expressions of God's creativity, and I treat others with all the honor that I would great masterpieces, for indeed we are.

I rejoice in every expression of life I perceive. The song of a bird, the beauty of a mountain, the fragrance of a flower, the softness of a kitten's fur all give me reasons to celebrate life.

> "The whole multitude of the disciples began to praise God joyfully with a loud voice for all the deeds of power that they had seen."
> —Luke 19:37

Day 91

—◆—

God's love satisfies every longing of my soul.

SATISFIED SOUL The yearning of my spiritual nature is an inner urging directing me to be fully aware of the presence of God. And so I pray:

"Thank You, God, for Your unlimited love, which feeds my soul and satisfies my every longing. I let Your love guide me today.

"A satisfied soul blesses me in all ways. I eat the right foods in the amounts needed for the nourishment of my body temple.

"My relationships are satisfying ones, for I do not seek in them what only You can give. They are enhanced as I give from a boundless wellspring of love within.

"Because my soul is satisfied with Your love, I make good use of the riches of the Kingdom. Thank You, God, for Your steadfast love, which feeds my every hunger and brings me joy and gladness all my days."

"Satisfy us in the morning with your steadfast love."
—Psalm 90:14

Day 92

—◆—

God protects and guides me.

NEVER ALONE — If ever I feel lonely or alone, there is One who will listen to me and comfort me. God will listen and respond in love and kindness.

I have only to become aware of God's presence within me to feel an overwhelming surge of warmth and love. God's presence is always within me, ready to comfort me. I know I am not alone.

If I am in a situation where I feel insecure, I affirm that God is protecting and guiding me in safe and successful ways. I am confident that I will come through this experience strengthened and renewed.

I talk to God in prayer, releasing all that concerns me. I know that God listens and then speaks to me through thoughts and ideas that clearly show me the way. I know what to do, and I have the strength to do it.

> "Let me . . . find refuge under the shelter of
> your wings."
> —Psalm 61:4

Day 93

—◆—

The Holy Spirit fulfills me.

HOLY SPIRIT

Does there seem to be something missing in my life? Perhaps there is some void that I have tried to fill, but the more I have tried, the bigger that empty feeling became. What I may be thirsting for is the Holy Spirit, which will fill any emptiness that I am experiencing.

Jesus told of a "living water" that satisfies every thirst. This living water is available to all; it is the Holy Spirit.

The cup that I hold to be filled is formed from my understanding of myself as a spiritual being—one who is receptive and open to the activity of God. I am not concerned about the size of my cup or the degree of my thirst, for I am drawing from a wellspring that never runs dry.

"Those who drink of the water that I will give them will never be thirsty. The water that I will give will become in them a spring of water gushing up to eternal life."
—John 4:14

Day 94

—◆—

*Praise God for a healthy,
strong heart!*

**A
STRONG,
HEALTHY
HEART**

Thank God, I do not have to continually think about my heart to keep it active. It goes on beating, sending life-blood throughout my body.

Yet I do know that the thoughts I think, the emotions I feel have an effect on my heart. Because I want to bless my heart, I think thoughts that are peaceful and positive. I do not add stress to the work of this wonderful organ. I cooperate with my heart by blessing it in prayer—spiritual exercise that strengthens my heart.

Every day I devote time in prayer to blessing my heart. Then I can go about my day giving my attention to what is before me to do. And I do it with all the enthusiasm that a healthy heart instills in me.

Praise God for a healthy, strong heart!

"Let the one who believes in me drink. As the
scripture has said, 'Out of the believer's heart shall
flow rivers of living water.' "
—John 7:38

Day 95

—◆—

God is my source of wisdom. I trust God to reveal right answers.

MY PATH

At times, my path in life may be marked by unexpected turns. These new directions, however, do not concern me. God is my source of wisdom, and I trust God to reveal the way.

God's guidance comes to me daily in the quiet of prayer. When I am quiet, I am receptive and alert to divine ideas. I follow God's guidance without resistance or doubt.

A particular way may not be the way I expected to go; but I am willing to follow where God leads me.

No matter where I go, I know that I will be blessed. God will only lead me on paths of great discovery and fulfillment. I am calm and capable because I know that God is with me. I come through every experience strengthened and enriched.

> **"The Lord will guide you continually,**
> **and satisfy your needs in parched places."**
> **—Isaiah 58:11**

Day 96

—◆—

Each day is a new day because I am growing and unfolding.

GROWING AND UNFOLDING Why is it difficult sometimes to forgive others? Is it because what they did was so unforgivable? Or is it because *I* have become attached to negative memories through continually thinking about them?

Releasing the past is the first step toward complete forgiveness. I can let go when I realize that the words and actions of others are responses from their own beliefs and responsibilities—not mine.

I am growing and unfolding at my own rate, in a world where no two people think or feel in exactly the same way. Knowing this, I release the need to force everything or even anything to happen the way I think it should. I am growing and unfolding, so I trust the divine order at work.

God's love assures me that, regardless of the past, there is nothing I have done that can keep me from a new beginning.

"You must forgive."—Luke 17:3

DAILY WORD

Day 97

Divine order is constantly bringing about change in my life.

CHANGE

One thing I can be sure of about life: It is constantly changing. Just when everything seems to be going smoothly, I can suddenly be confronted with a detour.

Change may make me feel unsteady or unsure of myself. My confidence is quickly restored when I turn the situation over to God. By reminding myself that God is in charge, I am agreeing with this truth: Change contains the seed of something that will enrich my life.

Change is *not* something to fear. It simply means that, for the moment, I am taking a different course. I look at change expectantly when I know that God is with me through every circumstance.

As I learn to welcome change, it becomes easier for me to flow with it. I know that God is in charge, and all is well.

> "Therefore we will not fear, though the earth
> should change."
> —Psalm 46:2

Day 98

—◆—

*My activities lead me to my
God-appointed place.*

POSSIBILITIES

Have I ever felt that I was standing at a crossroad and did not know which way to turn? I may have felt as if I were being pulled in different directions by outer influences. Whenever I experience such feelings of uneasiness, I turn to God in prayer and find relief.

Centered in prayer, I begin to feel my oneness with God and a renewed awareness of my connection with God's perfect order. I realize that divine order is always present, moving throughout my mind and body.

Even though I may not see it, divine order is always present and dynamic. I begin to understand that each activity leads me to my God-appointed place—a place that is especially for me and that is charged with limitless possibilities.

**"I am with you in spirit, and I rejoice to see your morale and the firmness of your faith."
—Colossians 2:5**

Day 99

—◆—

I am a radiating center
of divine love.

**DIVINE
LOVE**

Because I am a radiating center of divine love, love fills me and flows out from me to others.

Love shines in my thoughts, lifts my heart, heals my body, and fills my life. I am divinely irresistible, for love is a magnet that draws blessing after blessing to me.

I radiate love. Wherever I go, whatever I do, I am a blessing to myself and others. Divine love is "a lamp to my feet and a light to my path."

I love all of God's creations, seeing in each one the glory of God's spirit. I bless and encourage all who come into my life.

The radiance of divine love shines in me, for me, and through me to bless my world. I am a radiating center of divine love, and I am thankful to God for this glorious gift of love.

**"This is my commandment, that you love one another
as I have loved you."
—John 15:12**

Day 100

—◆—

My faith is unshakable,
for it is anchored in God.

ANCHOR OF THE SOUL
This may be a time in life when I seem to be adrift—tossing about like a ship in a storm. I may even feel as if there is no way out of the challenges at hand. Yet my faith in God assures me that there is always a way, for I know that with God, nothing is impossible.

In any time of doubt or confusion, I direct my thoughts to God and entrust my life and affairs to God's infinite love, wisdom, and power. God is my help in every need, and together, God and I can weather every storm. I know without a doubt that I have a refuge in God, a safe haven where I am protected and at peace.

As I rest in God's infinite love, I am uplifted; nothing can disturb the calm peace of my soul.

"We have this hope, a sure and steadfast anchor of the soul, a hope that enters into the inner shrine."
—Hebrews 6:19

Day 101

—◆—

I greet each day with a joyful heart.

JOYFUL HEART

Words of joy remind me that joy is part of my spiritual heritage. As I speak out with joy, I claim my heritage of happiness, peace, and joy.

Whatever I am doing, I determine to do it with a joyful heart. I know that I will receive more joy than I give, for this is divine law: "Give, and it will be given to you. A good measure, pressed down, shaken together, running over, will be put into your lap; for the measure you give will be the measure you get back."

Joy is like a mighty river—constantly flowing from God through me and uniting with the joy of people all around me. Together we enfold our world in joy.

I let the wellspring of joy flow freely from me so that I can be an open channel for even greater gladness. Out of that joy, I discover that my activities are meaningful experiences, and people are my friends.

"You have put gladness in my heart."
—Psalm 4:7

Day 102

—◆—

*I let go and let God take charge
of my life.*

**LET GO,
LET GOD**

What do I do when a problem seems unsolvable? I let go and let God show me that there is a solution.

If I am uncertain about the future or having difficulty releasing the past, I am not troubled. I know God is with me *now*. I let go and let God guide me in this present moment.

I let go worries or concerns about how I think something *should* be done and let God guide me to the *best* way to do it.

I do not become overwhelmed by the number of tasks before me. Rather, I let God's spirit lead me, step-by-step, to a new life of happiness and fulfillment.

God will never fail me. As I let go and let God take charge of my life, I realize that what seems to be an obstacle is, in fact, an opportunity for new blessings in disguise.

**"I will never leave you or forsake you."
—Hebrews 13:5**

Day 103

—◆—

The peace of God soothes my mind and emotions. I am serene.

PEACE OF GOD

Perhaps I have thought of myself as easily upset or disturbed by what happens to me. I am liberated from such an illusion by understanding that the peace of God can help me respond to every person and event.

Negative thoughts and feelings can stay with me only as long as I give them my attention. I choose to let the peace of God within me direct my thoughts and feelings. The power of God's peace is greater than any demands of life.

As the peace of God fills my mind and heart, I am inwardly serene and outwardly poised. Peace glows within me at all times and under all circumstances.

I let peace prevail, and in so doing, I maintain a positive attitude and a serene disposition. I meet life with grace and good humor through living every moment in the peace of God.

"Blessed are the peacemakers."
—Matthew 5:9

Day 104

—◆—

The Holy Spirit is my true security.

SECURE

Challenges will appear and disappear throughout my life, both in times of success and disappointment. Yet it is through the ebb and flow of events, habits, and attitudes that growth takes place.

Leaving the security of a familiar place, relationship, or comfort zone need not make me anxious. I can look beyond the temporary security that a situation or person offers and call upon my true security: the Holy Spirit. The presence of the Holy Spirit goes with me to all places at all times.

I am thankful that each opportunity to emerge from outgrown or inappropriate ways frees me a little more. I accept new situations with faith and eagerness.

As I welcome the guidance of the Holy Spirit, I find the strength and wisdom to make the most of each day's opportunities.

"Do not judge by appearances, but judge with right judgment."
—John 7:24

Day 105

—◆—

With God's help, I release the past and live in the now.

N o w !

Today's statement is one that I accept as true for me. By accepting God's presence in my life, I am able to release the past rather than relive it. The past cannot control my life because I release it now!

Holding on to hurtful memories would take me down a road that leads nowhere. So I choose a new direction. I turn from a nowhere destination to live in the here and now. I give prayerful attention to thinking positively and focusing on the present moment.

Today is a new day—a day in which I discard the baggage of old habits and limitations. I start anew with God. Following divine guidance, I know how it feels to be spiritually alive and in control of my life! I am open and receptive to all the blessings that God has to offer.

"Everything old has passed away; see, everything has become new!"
—2 Corinthians 5:17

DAILY WORD

Day 106

—◆—

Through God's love in me, I am able to honor all my commitments.

COMMITMENT

Making a commitment may seem easy, but sticking to it can be a challenge. Even the most desirable new possibility requires continuing effort. If I am not ready to do my fair share of giving as well as receiving, of sharing responsibility as well as rewards, then I may not be ready to make a commitment.

Whether I seek a new job, better health, a new or renewed relationship, or greater spiritual understanding, I will receive from such a desire just what I am willing to give to it. Each day, I am sowing seeds from which I will reap a harvest of blessings.

Merely making a commitment promises me nothing. Fortunately, through God's love, I continually receive the wisdom, love, and strength to continue moving toward a worthy goal, to continue to honor all my commitments.

"Give, and it will be given to you."
—Luke 6:38

Day 107

—◆—

In silence, I am renewed.

RENEWED   I find rest and renewal in the silence of prayer. This is because, in prayer, I am consciously increasing my awareness of God. Prayer recharges my spiritual battery, and I am revitalized.

Each time I pray, I am immersed in divine love and peace. Any leftover tension vanishes, for I am in the presence of God. People or situations or circumstances that may have troubled me earlier no longer seem threatening. I give every concern over to God, and I trust God to take care of it all in the perfect way.

In silence, I become still and listen. God speaks to me through divinely inspired thoughts. Realizations come to me for the best ways to work through a challenge or to achieve a goal. As I turn within to the silence, God truly does renew me.

> **"But those who wait for the Lord shall renew their strength."**
> **—Isaiah 40:31**

Day 108

—◆—

*I can be the person I truly desire
to be.*

**TRUE
DESIRE**

What if I wake up one day feeling disappointed because I am not the kind of person I am capable of being? I may think that it is too late to change, that it is too late to be the person I know I can be.

In God's world, it is never too late. I am not living in the past; I am living in the *now*. God has created a pattern of perfection within me, and I can begin to express it more each day.

God's spirit whispers, "You can be all you desire to be." This loving spirit within me encourages me to know and accept that I can be more vibrant and loving, that my life can be more fulfilling.

I begin this day to follow the promptings of my spiritual guidance. I let go the beliefs that have limited me and become all that I am created to be.

**"Sleeper, awake! Rise from the dead."
—Ephesians 5:14**

Day 109

—◆—

The love of God heals me.
I am well and whole.

GOD HEALS ALL God heals not only the physical ills of the body but the emotional hurts of the heart and mind also. I give thanks for God's healing love, which is in my heart at this very moment, cleansing and removing all sense of injury or hurt.

In order to help God help me, I stop nurturing hurt feelings. I am willing to let go of resentments. If I should be reminded of a past hurt, I tell myself: "This has been the cause of enough suffering. I no longer give it a place in my life and thinking. The love of God sets me free from this experience and from the memory of it." I then fill my mind with the blessings that are mine from this moment on.

The love of God heals every cell of my being. My heart is filled with thanksgiving for the peace and serenity I experience.

"For he has delivered me from every trouble."
—Psalm 54:7

Day 110

—◆—

I accept the gift of life from God and make the most of it.

GIFT OF LIFE Life is a wonderful and precious gift. I continually keep in mind the Giver of the gift and remain ever grateful that the gift of life is mine to live.

What do I choose to do with the life that God has given me? I live it fully and freely by being the very best person I can be. I speak and act with love and compassion. I center my attention on the love of God for me and within me. I infuse everything I think, say, and do with love.

The life of God resonates from me more clearly each day as I honor it and let it express through me. I find that every moment of my life has meaning and purpose.

With a grateful heart, I say: "Thank You, God, for Your perfect life, which is within me now and always. I accept the gift of life and make the very most of it."

> "In him was life, and the life was the light of all people."
> —John 1:4

Day 111

—◆—

I take a serenity break to keep in touch with spiritual truths.

SERENITY

Every day I see or hear reports by the news media of crises the world over. I may listen to everything that is wrong in the lives of my friends, neighbors, and associates and feel overwhelmed.

So I make sure that I build several serenity breaks into my day. In these times of quiet reflection, I review the truth that is above and beyond current situations and circumstances. I think about God's presence, power, and activity in me, in the people I know, and in people everywhere.

My serenity breaks not only put me in touch with spiritual truths for all people, but also renew my own faith, strength, and wisdom. I act creatively in cooperation with the divine plan for all, and I renew this commitment each day wherever I am and in all that I do.

"In every place your faith in God has become known."
—1 Thessalonians 1:8

Day 112

——◆——

God's spirit is guiding me to my own right place.

RIGHT PLACE

If I take a look at who and where I am today, I may feel that I have fallen short of my aspirations and desires. If I am not using my full capacities, I might even feel that I am not in my right place.

How do I know where my right place is? My right place is the place where I feel in harmony with myself and with my world, where I am giving what I have to give in ways that bless me as I bless others.

In my right place, my life is evolving from the inside out. There is no circumstance or person who can deny my personal progress when it is the harvest of inner spiritual growth.

God has given me power and potential. Through prayer and faith, I call upon this power and potential to move into my right place. As I do, new and more abundant blessings are drawn to me.

"You guide me with your counsel."
—Psalm 73:24

Day 113

—◆—

The presence of God is with me at all times and in all places.

LOVING PRESENCE   Whatever challenge I may meet, I do not have to meet it alone. I do not have to go through anything alone, for God is a loving presence that is always with me!

If ever I feel separate from the presence of God, I say aloud or silently, "God is with me now." I affirm this truth again and again until I begin to feel God's loving presence. I affirm this truth until a new realization of my oneness with God sweeps over me.

I remember that I am not alone now, nor will I ever be alone. In the heights or in the depths of experiences, God is with me.

God is with me at all times and in all places.

Wherever I am, God is.

Wherever I go, God goes with me.

Whatever I have to do, God is working through me to accomplish great things.

"You . . . are in me and I am in you."
—John 17:21

Day 114

———— ◆ ————

Divine life flows through me as radiant health.

DIVINE LIFE

What a marvelous realization today's statement inspires within me. The life of God is in every cell of my body, creating new health! Knowing this, I live my life from a center of wholeness that is the very foundation and sustainer of life.

What if at times I feel less than healthy and whole? I still claim my health and wholeness through the life of God within me. Divine life is the health and strength I need to overcome any adverse condition of mind or body. I replace any thoughts of lack or limitation with thoughts of strength and renewal. Then I am able to envision my body as whole and free.

Daily I affirm: *Divine life flows through me as radiant health, and I am renewed in mind, body, and spirit.*

> "Paul . . . seeing that he had faith to be healed,
> said in a loud voice, 'Stand upright on your feet.'
> And the man sprang up and began to walk."
> —Acts 14:9–10

Day 115

—◆—

The door to new blessings stands open before me.

OPEN DOOR

It may seem at times as if a door I had wished to enter has been closed to me. Perhaps I did not receive the employment I desired, a relationship has dissolved, or some other situation occurred that forced me to change direction.

At times such as these, it is important for me to reaffirm the truth: God is the only source of blessings. I live this truth by knowing that no person or circumstance can take my blessings from me. Whenever one door closes, it is a signal to me that another one—a wider one—is opening somewhere so that greater blessings will be available to me.

I can find happiness and fulfillment in spite of change, for change opens doors that I did not know existed. Change brings great opportunities for blessings when I am ready and willing to be blessed.

"Look, I have set before you an open door, which no one is able to shut."
—Revelation 3:8

Day 116

—◆—

*I am healed by the power
of the Holy Spirit.*

**I AM
HEALED**

Through the power of the Holy
Spirit, my body is constantly being
healed and renewed.

Divine power is within me, and it
strengthens and renews me. Because this is the truth
about me, I focus my attention on this inner Spirit, not
on outer appearances. My mind and body are made
whole and free.

I am healed by the power of the Holy Spirit. I have faith in
the Holy Spirit as an undeniable healing power coursing
through me at all times. Each cell, fiber, and muscle of
my body works together harmoniously and efficiently.

I am healed by the power of the Holy Spirit. I feel such
spontaneous joy because I know that health is mine. I
am filled with peace, for I am healed by the power of
the Holy Spirit.

"Do you not know that your body is a temple of the
Holy Spirit within you, which you have from God?"
—1 Corinthians 6:19

Day 117

—◆—

As I let my mind, body, and emotions rest, I gain balance and new strength.

LET IT REST Sometimes, no matter how much I have to do, a few moments of rest will give me the boost to do all I need to do. And because I am paying attention, I know when my body is telling me to rest. So I rest.

If I am trying to resolve a difference with others and no resolution appears, perhaps the best thing I can do is to let it rest. By the time I next meet with them, the problem may have taken care of itself. If not, then I am refreshed and more alert to the right answers and actions.

Letting myself or a situation rest can be a great help. The very life and intelligence of God within the cells of my body communicate with me as I rest. The wisdom of God that I receive will influence every decision I make, every action I take.

"Come to me, all you that are weary and are carrying heavy burdens, and I will give you rest."
—Matthew 11:28

Day 118

—◆—

*All is in divine order, for God is
actively at work in my life.*

**DIVINE
ORDER**

There are many simple, yet revealing,
examples of divine order in nature. For
instance, a spider spins its web in an
orderly, set pattern and a seedling rises
gracefully from the earth and stretches its leaves toward
the sun—all in divine order.

I, too, am drawn to the light of divine order, which
establishes harmony in my life. If at times things seem
disorderly or chaotic, I make needed adjustments by
focusing on the presence of God and affirming: *All is in
divine order, for God is actively at work in my life.* My peace
and confidence are then restored.

I may not understand why events occur as they do,
but I can acknowledge that a greater plan is unfolding—
a plan of divine order—and I can draw strength from
knowing this. All is in divine order, for God is actively at
work in my life.

"Light will shine on your ways."
—Job 22:28

Day 119

—◆—

*I trust God to direct my words
and actions.*

How many times have I missed the true meaning in another's words simply because I was not really listening? And how many times have I been misunderstood for the very same reason?

Communication is an important part of every aspect of my life. In my relationships with others at work and at home, the success of the commitment may be determined by how well people communicate.

I learn to be a better communicator when I let God's loving spirit direct me. When I listen to others, I listen in love. I rely on God—not appearances—to show me the true meaning of someone's words or actions.

Trusting in God, I need never fear that I will be misunderstood. I am inspired to do and say the right things at just the right time.

"I will instruct you and teach you the way you should go."
—Psalm 32:8

Day 120

—◆—

I bless my body in prayer, and my body blesses me.

BODY TEMPLE

Within me, there is healing power that is unlimited in possibility and divine in source. I bless my body in prayer, and my body blesses me with strength, health, and wholeness.

My body is a temple for the Holy Spirit that dwells within me. From the top of my head to the bottom of my feet, I am filled with strength and energy. Every fiber of my being vibrates with life and energy. I feel recharged and revitalized, for I am being renewed every moment.

I give thanks for the beauty and wonder that make up my body—for the tremendous feats that it accomplishes daily, for the divine energy that it houses. I bless my body and my body blesses me with health. I rejoice, for I am vitally alive!

"Do you not know that your body is a temple of the Holy Spirit within you, which you have from God?"
—1 Corinthians 6:19

Day 121

—◆—

I am open to God's wisdom and love.

OPEN TO GOD

"Why did this have to happen?" I may ask myself this during times of challenge.

Although I may not understand the reason for some circumstance, I know that it cannot defeat me. A new day will dawn, and I will come through the challenge stronger and wiser because I am open to God's wisdom and love.

I recognize that God's love for me is perfect and can soothe all discomforts, mend any troubled heart, and raise every expectation above the circumstances. Any empty or sad feelings I may have had are soon replaced with feelings of love, comfort, and a true joy for living.

I pray with a grateful heart, "God, I am open to Your wisdom and love. Thank You for being with me, for guiding me and loving me in up times, down times, and all in-between times."

"Joy comes with the morning."
—Psalm 30:5

Day 122

—◆—

I make time each day for a prayer break.

PRAYER BREAK Throughout the day, wherever I am, I stop what I'm doing and take a prayer break. I don't need to close my eyes or wait for a few minutes of solitude. Wherever I am, whatever I am doing, I can still my thoughts and say a prayer of thanksgiving to God.

If something is troubling me, I release my concerns into God's care. The weight of a problem is lifted from me in such a time of close communion with God.

After my prayer break, I am peaceful and calm. Relaxed and refocused on the responsibilities that are before me, I know that I can do whatever I need to do in an orderly, efficient way. For a quick pick-me-up, I include a prayer break several times during my daily routine. It works!

"All these were constantly devoting themselves to prayer, together with certain women, including Mary the mother of Jesus, as well as his brothers."
—Acts 1:14

Day 123

—◆—

*God is with me—my comfort
at all times.*

**No
Greater
Friend**

I have no greater friend than God—a friend who is always there to listen, always there to comfort me. When I am troubled, God is with me, listening to my every word.

If I am grieving over the loss of something or someone, God tenderly holds my hand. If the pain I may be experiencing because of this loss seems more than I can bear, God carries my burden for me, loving me so much that I have love to share.

Such pain may not be completely diminished at first, but in time I learn to totally and wholeheartedly rely on God's active presence in my life.

I can draw upon the comfort and strength of God at any time. And I do.

**"I will strengthen you, I will help you,
I will uphold you with my victorious right hand."
—Isaiah 41:10**

Day 124

—◆—

*I breathe fully, taking in the energy
of life.*

BREATHE

There is something I can do to sustain and enhance the quality of my life that is easy to do—and it is free! I simply pause in whatever I am doing and breathe deeply and evenly.

Do I need to make an important decision, offer loving support to a friend, or release the tension of my day? I focus on God's presence within me, take a deep breath, and release it. Then I am ready to do what I need to do.

Any time I feel tired, I sit back for a moment, breathe deeply, and fill my body with life-giving energy. Feeling refreshed, I continue with my day.

Each breath of life not only energizes me but also reminds me of God's constant care and provision for me.

**"The God who made the world and everything in it . . .
gives to all mortals life and breath and all things."
—Acts 17:24–25**

Day 125

—◆—

In silence, I am filled with inspiration.

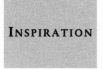

INSPIRATION

Am I searching for something or someone to help fill an empty feeling within me? What I am really searching for is soul satisfaction, and that comes when I turn within to God and wait in silence to be filled with divine inspiration.

In silence, I receive my inspiration quietly yet so deeply that I gain insights I have never before touched on or understood. An idea can bring a great blessing to me that I can pass on to others.

A soul filled with inspiration cannot be hidden away. There is a light that shines through me and spreads blessings.

God has an overflowing abundance of inspiration for all who will come in thought and prayer with an open mind and a receptive heart. And I do!

"I am the bread of life. Whoever comes to me will never be hungry, and whoever believes in me will never be thirsty."
—John 6:35

Day 126

—◆—

My thankful heart leads me to the riches of God's kingdom.

THANKFUL HEART

My heart is filled with praise, and I give thanks for all that God is so willing for me to have. Because I have a thankful heart, I am able to receive more of God's blessings in my life.

I am thankful for the wisdom and guidance that help me recognize the blessings that come through me and to me.

I praise God for divine life that heals and renews me. And I always have a reason to be thankful, for the revitalizing life of God is continuously circulating throughout my mind and body.

I am open to all the riches of God's kingdom. In fact, there is no blessing that I can possibly think of that God has not already prepared for me.

Abundance is mine! I give thanks for the unlimited flow of blessings into my life.

"O Lord my God, I will give thanks to you forever."
—Psalm 30:12

Day 127

—◆—

I bless others by knowing that the presence of God is within them.

BLESSING OTHERS

When I think of the people who have helped me the most along the way, I am reminded of those who saw something in me that I was unable to see in myself. These caring individuals, because of their faith in God working through me, helped me to have confidence in myself. My heart is filled with gratitude for each of these people.

As I think about them, I am reminded that life is about caring and sharing and that we are meant to be helpmates to one another. I pray that this day I will be a special blessing to others as I behold the presence of God in them.

Throughout this day, I will pay special attention and know when to offer words of encouragement or comfort. Seeing the greater good in others and giving expression to that good not only blesses others but also blesses me.

"You will be a blessing."
—Genesis 12:2

Day 128

*The powerful presence of God is guiding,
sustaining, and uplifting me.*

SAFE AND SECURE

God's spirit within me guides, strengthens, and sustains me despite any outer appearance of confusion.

Each day I have the opportunity to live and grow, to learn and teach, to love and be loved in this world. Yet, at times, I may face circumstances that do not seem to hold even a glimmer of anything that will enrich my life or the lives of my loved ones.

I don't give up or give in! Not when I know and affirm: *The powerful presence of God is within me.* This is a gentle reminder that God is always with me wherever I am. Blessings are unfolding around me, and each new day carries opportunities for greater growth, prosperity, and wisdom.

I know that the powerful presence of God is guiding, sustaining, and keeping me safe and secure.

"He led them in safety, so that they were not afraid."
—Psalm 78:53

Day 129

◆

A refreshing, healing flow of forgiveness fills me and overflows from me.

REFRESHING FLOW

An artesian well is a deep well—a well from which water flows up and out of naturally. It continually brings its fresh supply to the surface of the earth.

I have a well of forgiveness that flows from me as a movement of Spirit that renews me and all my relationships. It is natural for me to forgive, for the spirit of God moves through me as love and a willingness to shape something positive out of something that may not have seemed positive.

As I forgive, I am refreshed, for the spirit of God moves through me as a cleansing, healing flow. In the flow of God's spirit, every feeling of rejection, abuse, or misunderstanding is washed away. Forgiveness heals me and reaches out to others as an encouragement to acknowledge the spirit of God within them and within all others.

"Out of the believer's heart shall flow rivers of living water."—John 7:38

Day 130

—◆—

In a silent time with God, I know God's tender touch.

TENDER TOUCH

Entering into a silent time with God means turning away from outer activity, taking a deep breath, and fully relaxing into a state of calmness.

In silence, I go beyond quiet repose. I am ushered into a place of inner stillness where I commune with God. In this place of stillness and communion, I know the tender touch of God, which fills my body and stills my mind. I feel the warm glow of God's love rising gently within—soothing and healing my body, mind, and emotions. I know and understand God's unconditional love for me.

In silence with God, I remember who I am. I am filled with the peace that passes all understanding. From this place, I return to my daily living and savor the fullness of my life.

"Be quiet, for this day is holy; do not be grieved."
—Nehemiah 8:11

Day 131

—◆—

Centered in God, I discover all that I am capable of being.

DISCOVER Maybe others have labeled me as strong or sensitive, young or old, prosperous or lacking, healthy or sick. Yet I know in the depths of my being that I am more than a name, a label, or anything that a statistic can define.

So like Moses, I ask the question: "Who am I?" I ask not of others or even myself, but of the all-knowing presence of God within. As with Moses, God erases doubt about my strength or ability with the assurance that there is an all-powerful spirit of life and intelligence within me always.

Who am I? Each day, I discover more of who I am and all that I am capable of being as I experience the presence of God. Centered in God, I understand that today and every day is a day of discovery.

" 'Who am I that I should go to Pharaoh, and bring the Israelites out of Egypt?' He said, 'I will be with you.' "
—Exodus 3:11–12

Day 132

—◆—

*I am an expression of God's love
in my world.*

**LOVE
EXPRESSED**

I was created to be God's love in action. That bright spark of love within me was quickened at my birth. Expressing love to those who cared for me and about me, I allowed love to grow and develop in harmony with wisdom and good judgment.

Yet over the years, I may not have always responded to people and events with love. Then I forgive myself and others for mistakes that were made. I give myself permission to improve my relationships and to nurture new associations in ways that are better than the ones I used in the past.

As I faithfully remain aware of God's love for me and within me, I live my life with greater wisdom and from a sacred kindness. I am an expression of God's love for the world in my world.

> "The steadfast love of the Lord never ceases,
> his mercies never come to an end."
> —Lamentations 3:22

Day 133

—◆—

Through Your ever-present grace, God,
I am blessed.

GRACE

God, I thought I had seen unsurpassed beauty, yet You showed me more when a spectacular sunset spread colors across the horizon that I had never before thought possible. God, Your grace is so beautiful!

When I thought I had received all the love anyone could need, You poured out even more—through a myriad of people and experiences. Your grace is constant!

When I thought I had met an obstacle that there seemed no possible way around, You showed me a door and led me through. God, Your grace is so empowering!

Although my thoughts never quite measure up to the beauty, presence, and power of Your grace, thanksgiving lifts me to a higher perspective of how loving You are. God, Your grace assures me that I am loved and valued.

"From his fullness we have all received, grace upon grace."—John 1:16

Day 134

—◆—

I forgive fully and freely, and my mind is at peace.

CLEAN SLATE My mind is a wonderful instrument that has the ability to store all the information I choose to enter into it and the capacity to reexamine information at anytime.

If my mind should contain any negative thoughts and memories, I can release them now. I wipe the slate clean by forgiving freely and totally.

The power that people seemed to hold in my memories is gone, for I know that God is the one power in my life. I might not be able to change what has happened in the past, but I can choose to forgive, to let go, and to be at peace.

I move forward with a renewed sense of peace, for I am no longer burdened by negativity. Because I can and do forgive fully and freely, my mind is filled with a peace that sustains me through all circumstances.

"Whenever you stand praying, forgive, if you have anything against anyone."
—Mark 11:25

Day 135

—◆—

I dream the dreams inspired by Spirit and then act on them.

DIVINE DREAMER

Do some people say that I am a dreamer, hinting that I am something less than I should be? They don't know that I am using the tools of imagination and faith and painting a scene of something that is a real possibility for me. I recognize my dream as it takes shape, alert to the possibilities that are unfolding right before me.

Yes, I am a dreamer—a dreamer of what God has created for me to have and explore and share in this wondrous world. So I never let anyone, including myself, convince me that my dreams cannot come true, not when I know that they come from the divine ideas awaiting my acceptance.

I dream the dreams that are inspired by Spirit and follow them in ways that bless me and all those whose lives I touch.

> **"Jesus looked at them and said, 'For mortals it is impossible, but not for God; for God all things are possible.' "—Mark 10:27**

Day 136

I am united with others in a divine kinship.

DIVINE KINSHIP

Some people never seem to meet a stranger; they make friends easily. These people fairly radiate with warmth and friendliness, and it is only natural that they attract others to them.

I can share in this feeling of harmony with everyone I meet. In the company of my loved ones, I am generally relaxed and self-confident. When I take that same divine gift of harmony with me into my work environment, travels, and social settings, I spread friendliness.

When I view all people united in a divine kinship, I begin to feel more relaxed and willing to become acquainted with people I don't know. As I meet them in a spirit of goodwill, they will begin to feel comfortable and relaxed in my presence, and soon a lasting friendship will be formed.

"Blessed are the peacemakers, for they will be called children of God."
—Matthew 5:9

Day 137

I receive and give the gift of love.

GIFT OF LOVE

I have been given one gift that enhances all the other talents and abilities I may have. This gift is the love of God, the greatest motivator, energizer, and creative force in humankind, and I have been created to express it.

Love provides more beauty, exhilaration, and fulfillment than I can imagine, but this gift needs to be accepted and used in order to grow to its full potential.

When I nurture my relationships, my work, and my life with my own personal expressions of kindness and goodwill, I am giving the gift of love.

I create unique gifts of loving words and actions that nobody else can give in quite the same way I do. Love is my spiritual heritage, a special gift that I have been given and can share with others.

"We have gifts that differ according to the grace given to us."
—Romans 12:6

Day 138

—◆—

One with God, I let nothing disturb the calm peace of my soul.

CALM SOUL
Do I sometimes feel that outer circumstances keep me from experiencing peace of mind? Do I believe that to keep peace in a relationship I have to sacrifice who I am?

True inner peace does not come from a problem-free life or from sacrificing who I am. True inner peace comes from knowing my oneness with God.

I can experience this unshakable peace by becoming still and centering on the presence of God within me. I repeat the affirmation: *God and I are one,* and I begin to feel the peace that comes from knowing I am not alone, that God is always with me.

When I am centered in this peaceful, sacred awareness, I can choose to experience peace in every circumstance of my life. In every moment, I choose peace.

"Peace I leave with you; my peace I give to you. I do not give to you as the world gives. Do not let your hearts be troubled."
—John 14:27

Day 139

——◆——

Letting go and letting God, I create a true picture of my reality.

TRUE PICTURE

How do I let go and let God? The first step might be to imagine how it would look and feel.

Here is how the picture might look: I am relaxed—letting go any thoughts of a worrisome situation that may have been nagging me. I feel the relief as tension in my forehead vanishes and my mind clears. I let that relief spread down and loosen any tightness in my neck and shoulders. Now, I allow the relief to settle my stomach and flow down to the soles of my feet.

I focus on a closeup of my face—just look at how it radiates with peace. I know that the presence of God is within me and goes before me everywhere I go. I see all the people around me filled with the presence of God. Yes, I have created a true picture of letting go and letting God. Now I let this picture become my reality.

"God is my salvation."
—Isaiah 12:2

Day 140

—◆—

I open my mind and heart to learning and discovery.

LEARNING

What is just as sweet to the soul as honey is sweet to the taste? The answer, found in the book of Proverbs, is *wisdom*.

My soul craves wisdom so consistently that I am always open and receptive to learning that nourishes me in mind, body, and spirit.

I am able to understand what I read, see, and hear. I cherish all that I have learned and share it freely with others. Eager to learn, yet undaunted by how much there is to learn, I recognize that each new discovery is further proof of God's inexhaustible abundance.

The rich treasures of God's creation are always before me. Confident in God—the creator and source of all—I open my mind and heart to learning and discovery.

"The drippings of the honeycomb are sweet to your taste. Know that wisdom is such to your soul."
—Proverbs 24:13–14

Day 141

*I am filled with the joy and peace
of believing in God.*

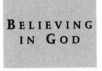

BELIEVING IN GOD

Watching the sun rise and fill the vastness of the horizon with light and color, I feel faith in God resonating throughout my being. As I look into the face of a baby and see the wonder of God's creation reflected back at me, I feel faith come alive in me.

And with such faith comes a reverence for the sheer magnificence that is God. The same Power that created a tiny infant is responsible for the rising of the sun and for all life.

As I survey the vastness of God's creativity, I surrender any feelings of doubt or insecurity, for the same Power that created such glory also created me. The kingdom of God is within me, and I am filled with the joy and peace of believing in God.

"May the God of hope fill you with all joy and peace in believing, so that you may abound in hope by the power of the Holy Spirit."
—Romans 15:13

Day 142

—◆—

I am awake to the possibilities life holds in store for me.

AWAKENING All of creation sings a song of life just for me. The earth is pulsating with life! Above ground I can see it; but even below ground I know it is there!

Like the earth, I awaken to the unlimited possibilities that life holds. I explore new ideas, experience new feelings, and embrace the wonder of discovery that is stirring within me and around me.

I weed out old ideas and feelings that prevent me from enjoying the entire landscape of possibilities. I clear the way for the growth of new ideas and feelings. As these ideas grow, I nurture them so that they take root and thrive.

This is a season of my soul; it is a time of awakening to new and wonder-filled possibilities.

"Sleeper, awake! Rise from the dead."
—Ephesians 5:14

Day 143

—◆—

I live the peace and happiness God created me to experience now!

LIVE NOW! I would never want to carry around all the material objects I have acquired over a lifetime. It would be impossible. Yet this is what I do on an emotional level when I refuse to let go of yesterday's mistakes and hurts. And I add to the burden when I take on concerns about tomorrow.

I can release any such burden and not take it up again. Today I invest my total attention in what is taking place now. I live the peace and happiness that God has created me to experience right at this moment—such peace and happiness do not rely on the past or the future.

To make each day count, I enjoy each moment. I can do this as I determine to let go fear and worry and live each day fully and completely in the now.

> "Teach us to count our days
> that we may gain a wise heart."
> —Psalm 90:12

Day 144

—◆—

I am thankful for the caregivers of the world.

CAREGIVER I may not remember the first step I took, my first day at school, or the first time I felt truly on my own, but I do have a real sense of how blessed I was by the people who loved me and helped me through these experiences.

Caregivers have held my hand, given me encouraging words, and offered me prayer support that helped me over the rough spots in life. Such support transcends the physical world and connects me in a spirit of oneness with loving, caring people.

The love of God is expressed by family, friends, teachers, health care workers, and all others who have helped me to know that I can accomplish more than I ever realized at the time. Yes, I am so thankful for caregivers!

"But we were gentle among you, like a nurse tenderly caring for her own children."
—1 Thessalonians 2:7

Day 145

—◆—

I celebrate and give thanks for the ever-renewing life of God within me.

HAPPY BIRTHDAY! Today is a very special day, for I dedicate myself to celebrating the "new me" that is emerging moment by moment.

I am grateful for each opportunity to learn and grow. Every opportunity to achieve and every challenge to overcome carries with it a message from the Spirit that I am ready, that I can climb ever higher.

My upward journey challenges me to be better than I have ever before realized I could be. Each new lesson in life renews me and revitalizes my interest in expressing the indwelling spirit of God in every area of my life.

Happy birthday to me! Happy birthday to everyone! Every day is a spiritual birthday, and I rejoice in each new opportunity to begin again.

"Love one another deeply from the heart. You have been born anew, not of perishable but of imperishable seed, through the living and enduring word of God."
—1 Peter 1:22–23

Day 146

—◆—

I envision God's perfect world—a world of beauty and harmony.

IMAGINATION

I can use my imagination to form mental pictures of God's perfect world as it was created to be.

I see people around the world living in harmony, one with each other and one with God. There are no borders and no limitations for anyone.

The earth is clean and beautiful. And it can be when people are good caretakers of the planet's natural resources and act in responsible ways.

I envision myself waking in the morning and facing the day filled with vim and vigor. I enjoy both physical and mental strength and vitality.

Now, through my faith-filled prayers, words, and actions, I turn my powerful mental pictures into reality. With God's help, I can do it!

"Let us then pursue what makes for peace and for mutual upbuilding."
—Romans 14:19

Day 147

—◆—

*The foundation of true strength is a gentle,
loving, nonresistant attitude.*

STRENGTH

Water in a stream yields to obstacles in its way, moving over rocks and around boulders in a continual flow.

So do I in my course in life. Whether I am working with an anxious boss or an energetic toddler, I have a far greater chance for success when I understand that nonresistance is a great strength.

When I am gentle, I retain a calm poise that is in my own best interest and in the interest of others. Then I am able to listen quietly and to empathize with the other person's point of view or feelings so that we can move toward an understanding or an agreement that benefits us both.

I realize the strength and wisdom that are required to be gentle and flexible and, most important, I realize that God is always giving me a fresh supply.

**"Show by your good life that your works are done
with gentleness born of wisdom."
—James 3:13**

Day 148

—◆—

Today I begin a journey of spiritual discovery.

SPIRITUAL JOURNEY Is there a longing in my soul for this day to be better than any other day I have ever experienced? When I believe it can be, I will begin a new journey—a journey in which I leave behind doubt and fear, regrets and guilt, and discover my spiritual nature and power.

I walk the walk of a triumphant child of God, for this is who I am. I talk a language of "I can!" which connects me with the truth of my indwelling strength and ability. I accept the reality of myself as a spiritual being on a divine quest!

Yes, I feel a rush of excitement about my journey. I know that God is my constant companion in my journey of discovery, and I will never lose my way.

> "Then those who went ahead and those who
> followed were shouting, 'Hosanna!' "
> —Mark 11:9

Day 149

—◆—

I am renewed, refreshed, and revitalized.

RENEWED

The radiant life of God is continually flowing through me, making me whole, well, and free of any discomfort.

If I find myself beginning to feel stressful about my well-being, I immediately refocus my attention on the healing power of God that is moving in and through me, renewing, refreshing, and revitalizing me. As I turn to God in prayer, fear has no hold on me and worries fade to nothingness. And the bonus for me is that I feel better!

During my prayers, I release myself into God's care and keeping. I gladly let go of all tension from my mind and body and immerse myself in God's wellspring of life.

I leave my prayer time refreshed and renewed. I am surrounded and sustained by divine love and know that God's will for me is being fulfilled now and always.

**"Those who wait for the Lord shall renew
their strength."
—Isaiah 40:31**

Day 150

—◆—

God enfolds me in love and peace.

ENFOLDING LOVE
Whatever this day holds in store for me, I know that I do not have to meet it alone. God is with me, providing me with everything I need to come through any experience feeling loved and blessed.

There is no problem that is too difficult for God and me to handle. Even when there seems to be no answer, I know that there is. God is my answer. I trust God to show me what is best.

As I listen quietly, I understand that I am invited to rest, to turn any problem over to God. A feeling of love embraces me, leaving me peaceful and calm.

God enfolds me in love and compassion. Even if it seems that no one in the world understands my feelings, I know that God does. God's unconditional love heals my heart and soothes my mind.

"Peace I leave with you; my peace I give to you."
—John 14:27

Day 151

—◆—

Thank You, God, for always being with me.

IN GOD'S PRESENCE

God, You are with me now, and I savor the joy of Your presence. In whatever challenge I am going through, You are with me. Nothing can come between You and me, between my blessings and me—not when I know the truth of Your love and caring.

Every burden becomes lighter, every day shines brighter, every expectation grows higher because I know You are my constant companion.

You never ask that I try to explain, excuse, or apologize for anything I have done or not done. You ask only that I leave the old, limited ways behind and step out in faith into new and better ways.

Thank You for always being with me, for guiding me, supporting me, and caring for me. I am safe and secure in Your presence.

> "But surely, God is my helper;
> the Lord is the upholder of my life."
> —Psalm 54:4

Day 152

—◆—

I remember others in my prayers.

REMEM-
BERING
OTHERS

It is easy for me to remember to pray for people when they experience a challenge, and I do. But I may not remember to pray for them when everything is going well.

So I make today and every day a day for giving thanks for all the people in my life. I am blessed with many special relationships—with family members, friends, co-workers, even those with whom I have only a passing acquaintance. Each time I encounter these special people, I am given a brand-new opportunity to bless them and receive a blessing from them.

As I pray for others, I expand my vision to include people around the world, people near and far who are part of my worldwide family. I love them and bless them and give thanks for their valuable contributions.

"I am grateful to God . . . when I remember you
constantly in my prayers night and day."
—2 Timothy 1:3

Day 153

—◆—

The spirit of God within me teaches me the ways of truth.

I Am Teachable

Infants are born with a hunger for learning. They absorb what they need to learn through all their senses. Learning is a joy for children, and every day is filled with wonders to be discovered. Yet such wonder is not just for children alone.

Regardless of age, I can discover the joys of learning. Jesus understood this and often used illustrations from nature or from everyday activities when He taught. He knew that everyone could learn from the simple things in life.

By listening to the spirit of God within me, I can learn more of the ways of God and the workings of divine law. Learning will be a joy for me, and my life will be filled with joyous wonder when I am willing to be taught.

> "Make me to know your ways, O Lord;
> teach me your paths."
> —Psalm 25:4

Day 154

—◆—

God is my prosperity—a prosperity that truly satisfies me.

GOD IS MY PROSPERITY Prosperity is never really about having an abundance of *things*; it is about knowing God and knowing that God has created an abundant world for us.

There may be a limit to the things I can claim as mine. Someone may build a bigger house, own a better car, or earn more money. However, the abundance of God is for everyone and satisfies every need.

To know God as a loving presence is to experience prosperity. To realize that God's spirit lives within me is to feel prosperous. To understand that God's spirit is also within my loved ones is to consciously share the good news of prosperity. To believe I am worthy is to be prosperous.

God is my prosperity—a prosperity of abundant blessings that satisfies every need.

**"I am going to bring it recovery and healing;
I will heal them and reveal to them abundance of
prosperity and security."
—Jeremiah 33:6**

Day 155

—◆—

I am one with a loving God and a friendly universe.

FRIENDLY UNIVERSE My awareness of universal friendship expands when I open my heart and mind to God's presence within me, within all life. I feel love, acceptance, and friendliness expressing in and through me.

Because I am aware of a spiritual oneness with God, I remain an expression of true friendship in the world. Thinking of myself as a friend motivates me to be friendly to everyone I meet. I am a positive influence, a spiritual friend to all, which links me mind, heart, and spirit to others. I can always be the very expression of the friend I want to be.

What a joy to be a partner in universal friendship! My routines become rich and satisfying as I discover new opportunities to share in the joy of living with others.

I am never alone, for I am one with a loving God and a friendly universe.

"I have called you friends."
—John 15:15

Day 156

—◆—

The unconditional love of God frees me to be
healthy and whole.

UNCONDI-
TIONAL
LOVE

One of the most health-promoting activities I can participate in is exercising forgiveness toward myself and others.

Through forgiveness, I free myself from the past so that I may more fully experience the blessings that are in my life right now.

Forgiveness removes the barriers in my mind that have seemed to separate me from God's healing love.

Forgiveness empowers me to create a life and a world based on the love, compassion, and kindness that God has given me to express in my life and my world.

I cannot change the past, but I can change the thoughts and feelings I hold about the past. And I can change the way past events affect me in the present.

"As God's chosen ones, holy and beloved, clothe
yourselves with compassion, kindness, humility,
meekness, and patience. . . . Forgive each other."
—Colossians 3:12–13

Day 157

—◆—

*God inspires me to achieve the highest thoughts,
words, and actions.*

**GOD
INSPIRES
ME**

In looking back, I may feel a twinge of embarrassment or regret about something I have thought, said, or done.

Well, many people have already gone down that path and welcome me to a world in which I am a living, breathing participant in life. Each day I am learning. Although some lessons may seem hard, I am growing in strength of spirit each day as I seek the guidance of God.

Allowing divine wisdom to guide me, I become wiser. So it is natural that when I do look back at who I was a year, a month, or even a day ago, I understand that I am different now. I am God-inspired, and divine inspiration encourages me to think thoughts, speak words, and take actions that are in line with the very quality of life I was created to express.

"These things God has revealed to us
through the Spirit."
—1 Corinthians 2:10

Day 158

—◆—

I say "yes" to giving God a chance to bless me.

GIVE GOD A CHANCE Have I been so busy trying to get everything done that I have not given God the opportunity to help me? God is my loving friend, a willing partner in a divine plan. When I turn to God within me and invite divine power to move in my life, I know that I will be immeasurably blessed.

Today, I give God a chance. I give God the chance to show me how wonderful life can be. I let go of the need to force something to happen and let God perform miracles in me and through me. I gratefully accept what God offers, for it is the best.

Each moment of every day is a new opportunity for me to discover more of God's blessings in my life. When I get myself and my own concerns out of the way and accept God's love and blessings, my life is enriched in every way.

"Whoever trusts in the Lord will be enriched."
—Proverbs 28:25

Day 159

—◆—

I greet each day as it is—a golden day filled with blessings!

GOLDEN DAYS

When did I last have one of those golden days when everything seemed perfect? I long for a day when every traffic light I come to is green, when something I especially need is on sale, or when the answer to an important question immediately comes to mind.

Such things may seem important, but every day can be a golden day when I am living it in an awareness of my own spirituality. Just as Jesus discovered the innate divine power within Himself and recognized His oneness with God, I, too, can do the same.

My inner divinity is real, for through the spirit of God within me, all things are possible. And like Jesus, I have the strength of faith to meet each day with great expectations of blessings. This is a golden day, and I greet it with great enthusiasm!

"One who trusts in the Lord is secure."
—Proverbs 29:25

Day 160

—◆—

*Laughter invigorates and
revitalizes me.*

HUMOR

How often have I been reminded,
"laughter is the best medicine"? And it
does feel good to have a hearty laugh
or even a gentle chuckle.

When I laugh, especially if I find something *very*
amusing, I am physically energized and invigorated.
The more I laugh, the more air I take in. As my lungs
work harder, so, too, does my heart—pumping blood
faster and revitalizing every cell and muscle of my body.

Mentally, I alleviate my mind of worry, stress, or
strain. All else is forgotten as my mind focuses on the
humor at hand.

The laughter I enjoy can also be shared with others.
Telling an amusing story can brighten someone's day.

Through the power of laughter, I am invigorated
and revitalized.

**"A glad heart makes a cheerful countenance."
—Proverbs 15:13**

Day 161

—◆—

As I listen, God lovingly guides me.

LISTEN TO GOD

When I ask a friend a question, I stop talking and listen so that I can receive an answer. In order to receive an answer to the questions I ask of God, I need to still my thoughts, open myself to divine guidance, and listen when I pray.

God hears my questions and provides the answers at the right time and in the right way. The answers I receive may not always be the ones I expect, but as I enter into my prayer time with an attitude of openness to a blessing and with faith in God's wisdom, I will receive the assurance for which I yearn.

As I listen, I feel an overwhelming sense of peace and well-being, for God loves me, hears me, and answers my prayers.

"Listen, children, to a father's instruction, and be attentive, that you may gain insight; for I give you good precepts: do not forsake my teaching."
—Proverbs 4:1–2

Day 162

—◆—

I live in the light of God's comfort and peace.

LIGHT OF GOD

Whatever confronts me today, I know that I am not alone. God is always with me, loving me and supporting me through every challenge.

I am God's beloved child, created for life in the fullest. I know that challenges are temporary, but God's radiant light shines constantly in and through me to bring order to my world.

I live in the light of God's comfort and peace. I rely on God's light to guide me and show me the way. I turn to God in every circumstance, for God will never fail me.

I accept God's peace into my mind and heart. Knowing the presence of God transforms my life, so that sorrow and doubt give way to joy and understanding.

As I give thanks for God's loving presence, I allow the peace that passes all understanding to soothe my soul.

"I am with you always."
—Matthew 28:20

Day 163

—◆—

I am the whole and holy being that God created me to be.

TOTAL BEING

Something powerful is stirring within me. It is more than a thought or a feeling; it is a certain knowing that I am a total being—spirit, mind, and body.

In the past, I may have felt as if there were something lacking in me or in my life. I may have even tried to appease this hunger for something more in my associations with people, in the accumulation of material things, or in attempts to achieve goals. But none satisfied my need.

Now I know there is more to me, more to life than I have ever before experienced. God's spirit is within me; I am a spiritual being. My yearning for more was my desire to know God, to be aware that God is always with me in all that I am going through. I am whole and holy, for God within me is my strength, my life, my hope.

> "If there is a physical body,
> there is also a spiritual body."
> —1 Corinthians 15:44

Day 164

—◆—

I give thanks for God's comforting presence in my life.

LOVING FRIEND

God is a loving, supportive friend whose door is always open as a sign of welcome to me. Day or night I can turn to God, my source of strength and harmony, joy and peace.

I call upon the healing power of God to energize and uplift me. The way to restored health is open before me, and I am immediately comforted.

I call upon God with prayers for my prosperity. I feel a surge of divine power that moves me toward new opportunities. God shows me the way to prosper and flourish, and I am at peace.

I can call upon the comforting power and grace of God at any time. With prayers of praise and thanksgiving, I bask in the beauty and wonderment of God's love for me, and I am filled with peace.

> "May the God of hope fill you with all joy and peace in believing."
> —Romans 15:13

Day 165

—◆—

I am blessed to be a part of God's glorious world!

GOD'S WORLD
How can I not feel the presence of God whenever I take the time to appreciate the beauty and wonder of God's world?

Whether I am listening to the sounds of the ocean crashing over rocks, feeling the tranquillity of a mountain lake, or simply observing the flowers growing in my own backyard, I experience a sense of wonder. Planet earth is my home, a home to a world of magnificent creations.

My heart is filled with joy and gratitude for I know that God, the creator of this glorious earth, also created me. I feel privileged to be a part of God's world.

Each day, no matter where I am or what I am doing, I take time to give thanks for the presence of God in the midst of the diverse and beautiful world in which I live.

> "The earth is the Lord's and all that is in it,
> the world, and those who live in it."
> —Psalm 24:1

Day 166

—◆—

*I dedicate myself to being an
instrument of God's blessings.*

MY BEST

God, when I am doing my best
work, I am using the wisdom, talents,
and abilities that You have given me.

So my prayer is that I never over-
look the importance of what I do or an opportunity to
do my best. I have something worthwhile to give and
so does everyone else.

God, if I am not already in the place where I can do
the best for my human family, the animal kingdom,
and the planet, I trust You will lead me to the place
where I can.

I may never know just how much I have helped
another of Your creations by being loving, thoughtful,
and caring, but I don't need to know. As I let Your spirit
work through me, I not only add to the quality of my
life, but I support the sacredness of all life as well.

"Commit your work to the Lord,
and your plans will be established."
—Proverbs 16:3

Day 167

—◆—

God's healing life renews my mind, body, and spirit.

TOTAL RENEWAL

A healthy person is one who is balanced in mind, body, and spirit, because each part is equally important in maintaining the strength of the whole.

So I do what I can to keep my mind and body strong—I eat right, I exercise regularly, and I stimulate my mind by trying new and different approaches to my everyday activities.

But how do I strengthen my spirit? I renew my spirit by turning to God in prayer. Prayer is the key that unlocks the door to every kind of healing. I am renewed in mind, body, and spirit when I let God help me.

As I rely on God's healing energy and follow divine guidance, I am strengthened and full of enthusiasm for life.

"For I will restore health to you,
and your wounds I will heal."
—Jeremiah 30:17

Day 168

I keep on keeping on in my spiritual quest for truth.

KEEP ON

There is a difference between releasing what is no longer in my best interests and giving up on someone or some opportunity. When I let something go, I am giving it to God to use in a way that will bless me and others.

Whatever I need to release—heartfelt emotions, attachment to a person or place, even some object that is no longer useful—I give thanks for the blessing it has been for me and then surrender it to God. I realize that I do not need to hold on to everything; rather, I need to keep on keeping on in my spiritual journey.

In the spirit of my belief, I surrender all to God. With a steadfast, unwavering faith, I trust God to help me know what is right. I keep on keeping on in my spiritual quest for truth.

> **"The Lord stood near him and said,
> 'Keep up your courage!' "**
> **—Acts 23:11**

Day 169

—◆—

*I live and work in harmony
with others.*

**WORKING
TOGETHER**
A car engine is made of hundreds of different parts. Not all look alike or have the same function, yet all work together to perform in a way that seemed impossible a hundred years ago. And if one of those parts should fail to work in harmony, the entire engine can break down.

Like a part in a finely tuned engine, I work in harmony with others to make this world a better place in which to live. Although I don't look like others or live in the same environment, I can create harmony and peace within my own space.

If I greet others with friendship and love, then they will most likely respond in kind. This process can continue from person to person—each responding with kindness—until the entire population works together as one.

"Let all that you do be done in love."
—1 Corinthians 16:14

Day 170

—◆—

Freedom is an attitude of mind and heart that frees my soul to soar.

FREEDOM OF MIND AND HEART
The caged bird may be limited in where it can fly and what it can see, but its spirit soars freely as it sings its sweet song. It overcomes physical limitations and allows its true nature to come forth in a soothing song of peace.

True freedom is a gift from God, an attitude of mind and heart that frees the spirit to soar above appearances. It is a willingness to go forward in faith to do what God created me to do.

I am free! Thank God, I am free! I no longer allow doubts to keep me from trying something new. No one and no thing has the power to keep my blessings from me, so I am confident as I embrace the spiritual freedom that God has given me and to all.

> "Where the Spirit of the Lord is, there is freedom.
> And all of us . . . seeing the glory of the Lord . . .
> are being transformed into the same image from
> one degree of glory to another."
> —2 Corinthians 3:17–18

Day 171

—◆—

Wherever you are, I enfold you in prayer.

BLESSED BY PRAYER

At times—out of the blue—certain people pop into my thoughts. I may think of them, remember times with them, and then let them go. But today when I think of others, I give them a prayer blessing:

"Wherever you are today, I enfold you in prayer. I see you healthy, whole, and free, blessed by God in all that you do. If anything in the past has come between us and our relationship, between our friendship and trust, I now place it in the flow of divine love which always connects us.

"You and I are forever one in spirit. I know this when we are together and when we are apart. Each loving prayer I send your way reaches you on some deep level. You may not be totally aware of me, but you are blessed by my prayers. This is all I ask or expect of my prayers for you."

"Pray for one another, so that you may be healed."
—James 5:16

Day 172

—◆—

I am preparing for something wonderful!

SOMETHING WONDERFUL   I gently let go of the hand of the eager child who is ready to walk on his or her own. I release the seed to an environment that nourishes its growth into a sturdy plant. As I let go, I am affirming that God is going to do something wonderful through the child and with the seed.

Yet sometimes—especially in a crisis—I may think that I just *can't* let go, that there *must* be something more that I can do. Crisis or not, I *am* doing something when I let go and let God.

Letting go and letting God, I am being of help. I am saying: "God, here is the situation, the person. I believe that there is no limit to the life, love, and peace You can pour out. I believe nothing is impossible for You and through You. So in letting go, I am preparing for something wonderful."

> "If you are able!—All things can be done for the one who believes."
> —Mark 9:23

Day 173

—◆—

I pray that my loved ones know the presence of God in all that they do.

DEAR TO MY HEART

I send my loved ones this blessing: "You are dear to my heart, and my greatest desire for you is that you know the presence of God in your life. I pray with you and for you, knowing that what is best for you is not my will or your will; it is God's will.

"God's will is that you have life, understanding, joy, love, and peace. This does not necessarily mean that every day of your journey through life will be an easy one. When you need extra strength to reach some goal, God is your source of almighty strength.

"Yes, you are dear to my heart, but as great as my love for you is, God's love is greater. So I pray that in all that you do, you know the presence of God."

"We have not ceased praying for you and asking that you may be filled with the knowledge of God's will in all spiritual wisdom and understanding."
—Colossians 1:9

Day 174

—◆—

*Having faith in God, I am filled with strength
and assurance.*

**MIRACLE-
WORKING
POWER**

When I look around me, I see the
miracle-working power of God everywhere, in everything. When I am
looking at nature, I see the majesty of
God's work in every leaf and in every blade of grass.
If I am looking at buildings, roadways, or bridges, I
can see the divine creativity that inspired individuals
to build such complex shapes and structures.

After looking at God's bountiful glory in the world,
how can I not have faith that God is with me and
around me? As surely as the morning will break each
day, as reliably as the moon "chases" after the sun
through the night sky, God will be a part of me and my
life forever.

With an infinite divine power on my side, I face each
day with strength and assurance, for I have faith in God!

"Cast all your anxiety on him,
because he cares for you."
—1 Peter 5:7

Day 175

—◆—

I greet each turning point as an
opportunity for new blessings!

TURNING
POINT
There have been many different times in my life when I arrived at a turning point—a time of change. I know within my own heart and mind that each turning point is an opportunity to change my life for the better. Spirit is letting me know that now is the time to take action and to do my part.

Whether these changes come in the form of making a move from one home to another, beginning a new job, or starting classes at a school where I may not know anyone, I remember that God has guided me to this point in my life. Each turning point, although unique, is a chance to experience new blessings.

I meet these turning points with great joy and expectancy, for new opportunities await me!

> "Trust in the Lord with all your heart. . . .
> And he will make straight your paths."
> —Proverbs 3:5–6

Day 176

—◆—

I act responsibly and lovingly toward all of God's creatures.

ANIMAL BLESSING Acceptance, love, kindness, generosity—all these qualities can be true of people as well as the pets that share their lives. So I bless all animals in my prayers today, acknowledging that they, too, are being divinely cared for and loved by the same God that protects and loves all.

I give thanks for the pets who keep me and others company. More than just animals, they are beloved family members. These pets never need to be asked for their love and acceptance; they are given without question and without thought of return.

I do all that I can to create a loving, happy household for myself and my pets, acting in responsible ways toward them. I give thanks for my animal friends and the joy they add to my life.

> "God said to Noah, 'This is the sign of the covenant that I have established between me and all flesh that is on the earth.' "
> —Genesis 9:17

Day 177

—◆—

*I pray for my loved ones with heartfelt faith,
love, and assurance.*

**BLESSING
LOVED
ONES**
I include all people who are near
and dear to me in my prayers today for
life, love, and wisdom. I pray that they
are fulfilled in heart and mind. I pray
that they continue to know the peace and love of God
in everything they do and in all that they aspire to be.

"God, bless my loved ones with enthusiasm for life
and living. Bless them with prosperity in matters large
and small, and with strength of body and spirit. I know
that You are protecting and guiding them every day of
their lives. And, God, I thank You for the blessing of
their companionship and friendship in my life."

Today and every day, I pray for my loved ones with
heartfelt faith, love, and assurance.

**"If two of you agree on earth about anything
you ask, it will be done for you by my
Father in heaven."
—Matthew 18:19**

Day 178

---◆---

The peace of God moves out from me as blessing upon blessing.

THE PEACE OF GOD

I listen for a gentle assurance that all is well: It is the peace of God singing within me. As I am still, I feel a warmth that heals my mind and body: it is the peace of God circulating through me. I speak a gentle, forgiving language: it is the peace of God loving through me.

The peace of God is always within me, just waiting for any opportunity to be expressed through me in amazing ways. And the true wonder of it all is that as I let the peace of God sing, circulate, and speak through me, I am blessed.

Peace begins within me and moves out through me, infusing everything and everyone around me. As my awareness of inner peace continues to grow, so does my expression of God's spirit. Then what a blessing I am!

"Jesus said . . . 'Peace be with you.
As the Father has sent me, so I send you.' "
—John 20:21

Day 179

—◆—

Knowing that God loves me
strengthens and renews me.

GOD LOVES ME!

God loves me with a love that heals and restores, a love that transcends any other love that I have ever experienced or even dreamed I could experience.

I feel God's love emanating from deep within me as strength and hope, peace and wisdom. I recognize that I can never be separated from the love of God. So if I ever feel lonely or afraid, it is because I have left God out of my thoughts, not because God has left me.

I understand that any challenge is a learning experience that can be overcome and healed by the power of divine love. As I open my mind and heart to God's love, I am guided in a gentle, loving way. I feel a resurgence of joy and energy. I am strengthened and renewed, for I know that God loves me unconditionally.

> **"My presence will go with you,**
> **and I will give you rest."**
> **—Exodus 33:14**

Day 180

—◆—

Calling on God is my best action plan!

CALL ON GOD   I will never get a busy signal when I call on God. Always ready to answer my call, God lovingly lifts any weight of concern from me. There is nothing beyond God's ability to solve, correct, or heal.

The combination of my complete release of all to God and my complete trust in God brings about wonderful results.

The moment I call on God, I begin to think in calm, creative ways. Instead of thinking over and over about concerns and wondering when and how the right outcome will come about, I begin to know that it will and to think about how I will feel when it does.

Faith grows within me until I am filled with thanksgiving. I know even before I see the results that a blessing is on its way to me.

> "Cast your burden on the Lord,
> and he will sustain you."
> —Psalm 55:22

Day 181

—◆—

Through the power of God, I can!

I CAN! I may have climbed to the peak of a high mountain or gone to the top of a skyscraper and felt as if I were on top of the world. Or maybe there is an upbeat song that stirs my emotions every time I hear it. At these times, I experience such a rush of enthusiasm that I feel as if I can accomplish anything!

I can feel like this every day through the power of God in my life. With God's strength and assurance, I can begin each day with enthusiasm for all that I *can* accomplish, for all that I desire! The power of God is more remarkable than anything I could ever imagine, and I tap into that divine power each time I pray.

Through the power of God, I *can!*

> **"You have given them dominion over the works of your hands; you have put all things under their feet."**
> **—Psalm 8:6**

Day 182

——◆——

*In quiet moments with God, I
experience great strength and joy!*

**IN
SILENCE**

When I become quiet and spiritually
focused, I feel the thrilling reality of the
living presence of God. I am filled with
a deep sense of being loved, cared for,
and guided by the eternal life-giver and life-sustainer.

As I breathe deeply the energizing breath of life, I
relax. Every cell, nerve, and muscle rests in the warm
glow of God's nurturing presence. I am lifted above all
cares and concerns.

In communion with God, I receive the answers I
seek, along with the comfort, healing, and assurance of
continuing blessings of grace.

In my quiet time with God, faith, love, and wisdom
rise up to greet me so that I can return to the challenges
and delights of living with great strength and joy!

"You show me the path of life.
In your presence there is fullness of joy."
—Psalm 16:11

Day 183

—◆—

In sweet surrender, I turn everything over to God.

Sweet surrender is an attitude of mind and heart, an attitude of acceptance of blessings. When I turn *all* over to God in an act of surrender, I know true serenity.

Whatever I give to God is healed and made right, so I surrender any tendency toward negative thoughts or habits. What a relief it is to know that I don't need to struggle, that God is my strength and conviction. I also surrender any need to find fault with myself or others and immediately relax into a state of peace.

I give to God any discomfort of body or mind, knowing that even conditions that have troubled me over the years yield to divine power. I now understand that the woman who touched Jesus's garment and was healed was reaching out in sweet surrender, and so am I.

**"Seeing her he said, 'Take heart, daughter;
your faith has made you well.' "
—Matthew 9:22**

Day 184

—◆—

I am loved and loving.

CIRCULATE LOVE One of the greatest motivators of people blessing people is God's love. When I let God's love be expressed through me, I know that I am not saying or doing something for the return I may get from it. With a loving attitude, I stir up positive feelings within myself and within others.

I am loved and loving. Love circulates through my mind and body. God's love for me and within me reaches out through me. Love quiets any anxiety, softens my voice, and quickens my actions.

Love lifts me above any challenge, giving me a perspective that helps me to understand my important place in life and the good I have to contribute. Whatever I think, say, or do, I want it to be with love. The love I give comforts, strengthens, heals, and motivates me and others.

"Let all that you do be done in love."
—1 Corinthians 16:14

Day 185

—◆—

I am a thriving expression of the life of God within me!

EXPRES-SION OF LIFE A healing can happen in an instant or it can happen over a period of time. So my prayers, thoughts, conversation, and actions are all a part of my continuing health plan.

Prayer is my conscious connection with the life of God within me. In prayer, I speak aloud or silently, claiming the health that is mine.

My thoughts are a continuation of my prayers. So as I go about my day, I keep in my thoughts the same faith-filled, life-affirming words I have used in prayer.

My words are audible signals of my inner conviction. My conversation is about life and health for me and for others!

My actions are a reminder to all that I am a thriving expression of the life of God within me.

"Whatever you ask for in prayer, believe that you have
received it, and it will be yours."
—Mark 11:24

Day 186

—◆—

I have a divine connection with God.

DIVINE CONNECTION

This is a computer age of electronics where someone can sign on at a computer in one country and seconds later have a conversation online with someone in a country thousands of miles away.

As amazing as this may seem, there is something even more amazing. When I turn to my divine source in prayer, I go online with God faster than any computer hardware would ever be capable of making a connection.

I can easily go "live" and online with God throughout the day, wherever I am. With more miraculous results than human technology, God answers my questions even before I ask. The true information highway is a divine one that leads to God.

In my prayers, I go online with God and make a divine connection.

**"The same Lord is Lord of all and is generous to
all who call on him."
—Romans 10:12**

Day 187

$-\blacklozenge-$

*With God's help, my dreams become
a reality!*

GO FOR IT! Have I ever regretted not doing something? Maybe I did not try for a promotion I truly wanted because a test was required and "test" is another word for stress for me. Or maybe fear of rejection kept me from getting involved in what looked like a promising relationship.

Why hesitate when I feel something is right for me to do? God will be there for me and will give me the pat on the back that I need to strengthen my inner resolve if I should begin to falter.

If a mountain stands in my way, I climb it. If a river flows between me and where I need to be, I build a bridge to get across it. Nothing can stand in the way of my dreams with the power of God to back me up.

With God's help, my dreams become a reality!

"You will say to this mountain, 'Move from here to there,' and it will move."
—Matthew 17:20

Day 188

—◆—

The presence of God shines light on my way.

GOOD NEWS   Each day can be one of celebration whether or not it is a recognized holiday, because every day I see more and more evidence of God's active presence in my life. And I take time each day to remind myself and others of this good news and to unite in prayers of joy and thanksgiving.

My beliefs and faith are the keys to my happiness and well-being. By believing in the power of God, I am adding hope to my dreams, giving purpose to my actions, and putting life back into my living.

A ray of hope and good news always shines before me as the light of God—a beacon that illumines my way and guides my steps. As I become focused and ever aware of God's presence in my life, I stand on the threshold of a new day—a new beginning filled with the welcome news of the glory and wonderment of God.

"You are the light of the world."
—Matthew 5:14

Day 189

——◆——

In my sacred space, I retreat to the presence of God.

SACRED SPACE I can create a sacred space in my mind where I retreat from the everyday activity and confusion around me and be totally in the presence of God. I begin to relax and feel peaceful and content. I linger in the glow of God's presence, secure in the knowledge that I am being constantly cared for.

Whether I enter my sacred space on a regular basis, at the same time every day, or if I tend to enter it only when I am feeling stressed, I know that the door to inner peace is always open to me.

I enter my sacred space with joy and enthusiasm, for I am aware of God's presence there. Troubles are left behind, and stress is a thing of the past. Once I connect with God, all anxieties are gone. I leave the sacred space to resume my day, refreshed, renewed, and revitalized. I eagerly greet the day!

**"In him was life, and the life was the light
of all people."
—John 1:4**

Day 190

—◆—

I am alive and filled with the vitality of divine life!

VITALLY ALIVE!

Vitality is mine for the asking, and I do so now by expressing what is true: My body is filled with the rejuvenating life of God! What I declare in thought and word, I stimulate within my own body.

I bless my heart and feel it pulsating with divine life. My heartbeat is strong and effective—each beat brings refreshing, revitalizing blood to every area of my body.

I bless my arms and legs and feel the revitalizing, renewing, divine power surging through the veins and muscles in them. I am strong and agile!

I bless my eyes, ears, nose, mouth, and skin. Each of my senses is alert and responsive whenever I have need of it. With all senses working together, I remain alert and aware of everything around me.

I am alive and filled with vitality!

> "There is . . . one God and Father of all,
> who is above all and through all and in all."
> —Ephesians 4:4,6

Day 191

——◆——

Inner peace promotes healing of my mind and body.

GOD ASSURES ME

If I am nervous or concerned about a situation or a loved one, I may get "butterflies" in my stomach—a nervous tension that only adds to my distress. So I understand that feeling at peace is important to me physically as well as emotionally.

The best way to release the mental and physical discomfort I am experiencing is to place any anxiety into God's care and keeping. In answer to my faith-filled prayers, an awareness of God's presence fills me with assurance. All thoughts of concern or apprehension are quickly dissolved.

Once all fears are gone, peace quickly fills the void left behind. My mind is at rest, my thoughts are serene, and my body is no longer tense.

I am relaxed and calm as I experience the peaceful presence of God.

"A tranquil mind gives life to the flesh."
—Proverbs 14:30

Day 192

—◆—

I have faith in God, knowing that with God, nothing is impossible.

FAITH IN GOD

A little faith goes a long way in clearing my mind, in restoring inner peace, in allowing me to function as a person who is capable of great things, for indeed I am.

Faith in God in me and in others develops courage, patience, understanding, hope, and so much more. It strengthens me and every aspect of my life. Each thought or act of faith is like a single fiber that, when woven together with others, creates a lifeline that connects me to health, peace, prosperity, and great opportunities.

I have enough faith that keeps me going when there seems no way to go on. Such faith is the understanding that God will see me through whatever it is that I am experiencing. Faith is surrendering to God's presence and power and accepting that with God, nothing is impossible.

> **"If you have faith the size of a mustard seed . . .**
> **nothing will be impossible for you."**
> **—Matthew 17:20**

Day 193

—◆—

I am alive with life!

ALIVE WITH LIFE! God, my expectations of well-being can never measure up to the health and renewal that You have already created me to experience. Because I am Your living, breathing creation, I am alive with life!

Healing is a natural outcome of Your loving care and provision for me, and I am constantly being renewed. So I continue to affirm life in cooperation with the healing and renewal that are taking place in me now.

God, Your spirit lives in me, healing and renewing me. My eyes, my joints, my muscles, and my organs are alive with life. Life is an ever-renewing source of energy that moves throughout me. Healing happens naturally as the cells of my body are constantly renewed.

I am alive with life!

> "The Lord God formed man from the dust
> of the ground, and breathed into his nostrils
> the breath of life."
> —Genesis 2:7

Day 194

—◆—

My true reality is God's world—the real world.

REALITY CHECK It can be so easy to feel over-whelmed by a workload in which there seems to be more to do than there are hours in the day to do it.

So how *do* I avoid feeling overwhelmed? Rather than worrying about how everything will get done, I take a reality check. My reality is in God. The household chores and the paperwork are not in charge of my life—God is.

I am aware of the real world—God's world! I settle back, close my eyes, and feel waves of divine assurance flow over me. I rest and relax in the comforting presence of God, and I feel an infusion of energy and a clarity of purpose.

With God strengthening and guiding me, I will meet the schedules and take care of the work—peacefully and in order.

> "Go into your room and shut the door and pray to your Father who is in secret; and your Father who sees in secret will reward you."
> —Matthew 6:6

Day 195

—◆—

Yes, God's spirit within me is healing and renewing me.

SOURCE OF LIFE
More powerful than any miracle drug available, God is my source of life and health. If I am feeling "under the weather," I can strengthen my immune system by nourishing myself with prayer.

If I do use the added support of medicine, I know that keeping my spirits up and maintaining a positive mind-set are essential to any health treatment.

I can also call on my friends and loved ones to pray with me. Just knowing that someone else cares about me and is praying for me is in itself a wonderful tonic.

Once my thoughts are strong and positive, I am able to release concerns and focus on my faith in God. God's spirit of life and love is actively healing my mind and body. I am healed and renewed!

**"Your light shall break forth like the dawn,
and your healing shall spring up quickly."
—Isaiah 58:8**

Day 196

—◆—

I feel such joy in giving thanks to God, the creator and sustainer of all there is!

THANKS-GIVING

Is it joy that stirs up thanksgiving within me, or is it my thanksgiving that stirs up inner joy?

I feel such joy that I cannot contain it when I catch a glimpse of the magnificence that is in every person and animal, every flower, tree, or mountain. It is the joy of thanksgiving within needing to be expressed.

How can I not feel a surge of thanksgiving when everywhere I look, in everything I experience, I recognize that God is present as creator and ever-present spirit of life. I can never take anyone for granted, never feel more or less superior than any other member of the family of God.

No, I don't hold back the joy or thanksgiving I feel. Like all days, this is my thanksgiving day, and as I give thanks to God, I experience God's joy.

"I will give thanks to the Lord with my whole heart."
—Psalm 9:1

Day 197

—◆—

The amazing grace of God strengthens and upholds me.

AMAZING GRACE
It is truly amazing how one minute I can feel "on empty"—drained of all energy—and then have a sudden surge of energy that enables me to complete some important project or task.

God's grace is even more amazing! It is a divine activity that is always with me because God is always with me. And the more I rely on God, the more I will see and feel God's grace at work.

Do I need to be healed? Then I turn to God and experience the grace of God working in me as renewing, restoring life. I feel the amazing power of grace as it supports and strengthens me.

Do I need a new life and a sense of purpose? I trust God to help me and show me the life I desire. Behold! The power of God's amazing grace is working for me!

"The God of all grace . . . will himself restore, support, strengthen, and establish you."
—1 Peter 5:10

Day 198

—◆—

I thank God for who I am now and for the true me that is emerging.

TRUE SELF

Who am I? What makes me who I am? Is it my surroundings or the people I associate with? Or am I a reflection only of how I was raised? If I am searching for my own identity, I know that as I look to the wonder of God, I will find my true self looking back at me.

The truth is that I am a child of God. Because I know in my heart that I am a loving and loved child of God, I can face the present and the future with a firm grasp of where I am going and who I am. I let go of who I have been in the past or things that I have done and thank God for the new person that I am now becoming.

"Thank You, God! Your love and support are all I need to let go of my old self and start over with a new and improved me."

> **"Create in me a clean heart, O God,
> and put a new and right spirit within me."**
> **—Psalm 51:10**

Day 199

——◆——

I am right now preparing for new and greater adventures in living!

I AM READY
Have I ever felt as if I were at an "in-between" stage in my life? Maybe I ended one project or relationship but was not ready to begin another. Yet at the same time, I felt as if I should be doing *something.*

My ability to free myself from the past does not necessarily mean that I am ready for the next step. It could be that I am moving into a time of preparation, a time of rest and renewal that will give me the strength to carry on.

If I feel guilty because I have not had time to begin or finish some project, I give myself permission to just "let it be" and enjoy this special time.

When the new beginning comes—and I can be sure that it will—I will be ready and prepared to succeed beyond my greatest expectations.

"Come away to a deserted place all by yourselves and rest a while."
—Mark 6:31

Day 200

---◆---

Like every divine creation, I am a unique work of Spirit.

WORK OF SPIRIT
Great works of art are considered prized possessions in private and national collections. And compositions of the masters of music remain "hits" for hundreds of years! Surely the beauty of the soul has been expressed in such works of art.

And just in case I have not realized it, I now know that I am a work of art also. Even more than that, I am a work of Spirit. God created me and only one me, so I am unique and special. No *one* can ever duplicate or replace me.

So whether or not the image I see of myself is one I think of as a work of art, I know that I am! And if I have not considered the people around me as prized creations, I take another look at them. As God's creation, every person is of irreplaceable beauty and worth.

> "Come to him, a living stone . . .
> chosen and precious in God's sight."
> —1 Peter 2:4

Day 201

---◆---

I release all to God and live fully,
joyously, and creatively today.

MEMORIES
Some of my memories are so sweet that I could live in them forever. Some of my memories are ones that I cannot wait to leave behind. Yet all my memories are from experiences through which I have grown wiser and stronger.

With every thought, feeling, word, and action of today, I shape the memories of tomorrow. So I give my attention to God and to making today the best day ever. If sad memories do creep into today, I bathe them in the light of love so that they fade away.

Many experiences have brought me to where I am right now. I am free to release everything to God and live today fully, joyously, and creatively. I see myself and all others as God created us to be—spiritual beings that remain whole and holy.

> **"This is the day that the Lord has made;**
> **let us rejoice and be glad in it."**
> **—Psalm 118:24**

Day 202

—◆—

I am tuned in to the peace of God.

MY SOURCE OF PEACE

Before I can use a computer, watch television, or listen to the radio, I first have to turn it on. Great information, entertaining programs, and beautiful music are mine to learn from and enjoy when I turn on and tune in to the right service, network, or station.

The concept of turning on and tuning in is true of my spiritual life as well. To experience and enjoy the peace of God, I need to turn on my awareness to it and then tune in to the divine source of it.

God's spirit within me is the source of peace that calms, uplifts, and nurtures me at any time and through any challenge. So in the middle of stressful or confusing situations, I can be at peace. There is no denying that the peace of God is within me and fills me with serenity.

**"To set the mind on the Spirit is life and peace."
—Romans 8:6**

Day 203

—◆—

*My loved ones are safe and secure in
God's presence.*

**IN GOD'S
CARE**

For many people, one of the most
difficult things to do is to leave a loved
one in the care of another—even long
enough to go about doing what they
need to do.

Whether they are taking children to day care, finding
a long-term care facility for a parent, or even leaving a
family pet in the care of a veterinarian, it is not easy to
leave them and not worry.

However, if I am going through such a challenge, I
can alleviate fear by holding thoughts of God's loving
presence always with my loved ones. Without this faith
in God, I could easily become overwhelmed with doubt
and anxiety, but with it comes trust and the assurance
that family and friends alike are always enfolded in
God's care and keeping.

> **"Be strong and courageous; do not be frightened
> or dismayed, for the Lord your God is with you
> wherever you go."**
> **—Joshua 1:9**

Day 204

—◆—

*God, I lean on You and discover
complete serenity.*

**LEAN
ON GOD**

God, I know I can lean on You, for
You care about me. So I let Your
strength support me and Your love
carry me. You are always here for me.

You will help me through any painful experience.
You are my eyes when I feel I have to turn away. You
are my ears when I cannot bear to hear what has to be
said. You keep my heart filled with courage and hope.

God, I trust in You, knowing that You will be there
for me, through thick and thin, in the best of times and
in the most challenging of times. You are my rock, my
fortress, my everything.

I lean on You and discover complete serenity. I am
Your child, and You will never forsake me. You are
always with me as my indwelling Spirit.

**"I am the way, and the truth, and the life.
No one comes to the Father except through me."
—John 14:6**

Day 205

—◆—

My relationship with God leads me into a new frontier of discovery.

NEW FRONTIER

Every time I pray, I deepen my relationship with God and understand more about God's unconditional love for me.

My expanding, growing relationship with God is open before me as a new frontier to be explored. I delight in my every discovery and praise God for what I am capable of doing and being. Each step I take, each new achievement moves me on into this great new frontier.

I cultivate my relationship with God by spending time in prayer. But I can also heighten my awareness of God through my appreciation of the beauty of nature, the magnificence of planet earth, and my body's own ability to heal.

Most relationships have their ups and downs, but my relationship with God is special. It leads me into a new frontier where I can discover true joy and lasting peace.

"I trust in the steadfast love of God."
—Psalm 52:8

Day 206

—◆—

Thank You, God, for filling my life with the joy of expectation!

WAKE UP! How wonderful it is to wake up in the morning with the realization that every blessing imaginable is possible!

When I awaken my own inner awareness of God's presence, I know that all blessings are not only possible, but probable! The chances for enriching experiences are unlimited! I could just walk through any door and easily discover another blessing.

I wake up to potential! With the assurance that God is actively blessing me with love, I eagerly greet the morning with thanksgiving and expectancy. My potential for living life to the fullest is being fulfilled each moment of this day! *Thank You, God, for filling my life with the joy of expectation.*

I wake up to God and wake up to blessings! Morning, noon, and night, I am ready and willing to accept everything God has in store for me. *Thank You, God!*

"Then you shall see and be radiant."
—Isaiah 60:5

Day 207

—◆—

I am in the zone of spiritual awareness with God!

IN THE ZONE

It is easy to become caught up in a sporting event in which athletes play so flawlessly together that they seem to do no wrong. Every move, every play seems to flow naturally and without effort. Into the game with every fiber of their being, these athletes are playing "in the zone." They become one with each other, one with the sport.

And wouldn't I feel great if I were "in the zone" every time I had a decision to make or anytime I had something of significance to do? *I can!* I can be "in the zone" 24 hours a day when I tune out distractions and tune in to God!

I tune in to God by stilling my thoughts and listening to divine instruction. In the sweet silence of prayer, I become aware of a feeling of peace and total well-being.

I am "in the zone" of spiritual awareness with God.

"The Spirit of God dwells in you."
—Romans 8:9

Day 208

—◆—

I am a free and whole person.

FREEDOM OF SPIRIT I am free from anything that would hold me back from expressing the light and love of God within me! I am free with the freedom of Spirit. Thank You, God!

Life-affirming statements and uplifting conversations are composed of the words of a free and whole person, and I am that person now. I honor the sacredness that is my wholeness—my mind, my body, and my spirit.

I am free from any kind of dependency. I am aware that what I take into my body, I am taking into a temple of the Spirit of life. I honor the life of God within me by keeping my mind and body whole and free.

Freedom of spirit emanates from deep within me out into every moment of my life. Knowing that I am a spiritually enriched being frees me to live my life in a world of great possibilities.

> **"The free gift of God is eternal life."**
> —Romans 6:23

Day 209

I am filled with the unquenchable joy of Spirit!

UNQUENCH-ABLE JOY There is a joy I feel that comes and goes in response to what is happening to me and around me. Yet I have a joy that is beyond what I feel as a response to people and circumstance. The spirit of God within me is my source of true joy.

Granted, I may go through experiences that leave me feeling sad and lost for a time. But the joy of Spirit is an eternal flame that lights my way back home to the love, understanding, and comfort of the divine presence of my being.

In the presence of divine joy, I am encouraged to be aware of the love, peace, and strength that are in me, in others, and throughout the world. I know true joy, the unquenchable joy of Spirit.

> "For you, O Lord, have made me glad by your work;
> at the works of your hands I sing for joy."
> —Psalm 92:4

Day 210

—◆—

I have a choice, and I choose God!

I CHOOSE GOD
If something goes "wrong," do I automatically wonder "Why me?" It is okay to wonder why something happened, but I do not let myself become so caught up in speculation that I take my focus off the realness of God.

God's loving presence is within me. So when situations occur that threaten to overwhelm me, I have a choice: I can worry about what is happening or I can relax and know that no matter what happens, God is with me!

Even in situations where there seem to be no choices, there are. One of the greatest choices I can make is to trust God. By choosing God, I am choosing to see something meaningful in whatever may occur, and what is most meaningful is that I am opening myself to God's love and goodwill.

> **"Choose this day whom you will serve . . .
> we will serve the Lord."**
> **—Joshua 24:15**

Day 211

—◆—

I rely on God to guide me every step of the way.

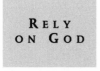

RELY ON GOD

Each day brings situations that require me to make decisions. Yet with so much going on around me, how do I know that the decisions I am making are the right ones? The right decisions come by listening to and following God's guidance.

So whether it is time to end a project or relationship or begin another one, divine guidance is only a heartbeat away. God speaks to me in every moment, but it is up to me to pause and listen, to rely on God to guide me every step of the way.

God speaks to me in many ways—through the still, small voice in my times of prayer and through the unexpected yet perfectly timed suggestion of someone. There is no limit to what God can do through me and through others.

"Teach me the way I should go,
for to you I lift up my soul."
—Psalm 143:8

Day 212

—◆—

*I seek God with all my heart and
I begin a new quest for truth!*

**DIVINE
QUEST**

Every quest is a search for meaning,
a search for God, so I begin my quest
by making the right preparations: I seek
God with all my heart—God's spirit
within others, God's presence within every situation.

At some point in my quest, I may need to step back
and give my life a good look, but I am ready and willing
to evaluate and decide what is worthwhile and what
needs to be changed.

Once I have a plan, I gather together the proper tools:
good judgment, a willingness to forgive, and unhesitat-
ing acceptance of all whom I may encounter. Above all,
I remember to love unconditionally.

Each new day is an opportunity to look for and find
blessings. Each moment is a new quest for truth, and I
am ready to begin my adventure now!

> **"If you seek me with all your heart,
> I will let you find me."
> —Jeremiah 29:13–14**

Day 213

——◆——

*The real me is a wise, healthy,
flexible, and free spiritual being!*

**SPIRITUAL
BEING**

Sometimes life can take on a surreal quality. I may feel as if I do not fit in, even with those I have been closest to in the past.

Well, if such times do occur, I do not doubt my realness, which is my spirituality. That feeling of not fitting in is an indication that I am a work in progress, that I am alive and living!

Yet the essence of who I am—my spiritual identity—never changes. I am wise, healthy, flexible, and free through the spirit of God within me. I do not have to conform to trends and fads—not the real person who I am.

And the real me never shrinks from learning new things. An awareness of my spirituality is such a confidence booster that I live and learn while remaining ever true to my spiritual identity.

The real me is a free, spiritual being!

**"Now we have received not the spirit of the world,
but the Spirit that is from God."
—1 Corinthians 2:12**

Day 214

—◆—

I free myself from the past by moving on into the now.

BREAK FREE

At times I may have a tendency to be my own worst critic about things I have done or "bad" habits that I have picked up. But if God never condemns me, then why would I ever condemn myself?

The past has no control over me. So if someone tries to hold me to past mistakes, I can break free. How do I do this? By moving on with my life and blessing that person, knowing that the past is merely a steppingstone to today.

Only God has power over me. When I declare myself to be free from negative habits, I free my body from the compulsions it had toward those habits. I give thanks that my body has the divine potential for renewed health and energy, which are continually being brought forth.

I break free from the past and begin to live totally in the now.

"Beloved, let us love one another."
—1 John 4:7

Day 215

—◆—

*Today and every day, I welcome the new me
I am becoming.*

NEW ME!

The person behind the reflection I see when I look in a mirror is constantly developing and learning from life, so much so that the person I see now will not be the same person I see the next time I look at my reflection.

With God continually molding me into a greater image—the divine image—I am always learning from my life experiences and from those of the people around me.

By watching, listening, and learning, I grow more spiritually alert every day. With learning comes growth and with growth comes change. Under God's care and attention, I know that I am changing for the better, for I am being transformed into a more loving, accepting child of God.

Today and every day, I welcome the new me that God has created.

"I will instruct you and teach you the way you should go."—Psalm 32:8

Day 216

I live and move in the presence of God.

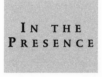

IN THE PRESENCE

Changing weather, urgent needs, and unexpected events may seem to cause me to make decisions I feel uncomfortable about making or may cause me to be in places I would rather not be.

Yet the important thing to remember is that wherever I am, no matter how far I travel or whatever the conditions may be, I am always, always in the presence of God.

This does not mean that I abandon good judgment, which is, after all, direction from God. If I am guided to stay put during a rainstorm or a snowstorm, I do just that.

But I do not live in fear of weather conditions or other circumstances. I live in faith in the presence of God.

> **"If I take the wings of the morning
> and settle at the farthest limits of the sea,
> even there your hand shall lead me,
> and your right hand shall hold me fast."**
> **—Psalm 139:9–10**

Day 217

—◆—

My heart is an instrument of God's love.

MY HEART

My heart is a powerful muscle that continually circulates life-sustaining blood throughout my body. In an awe-inspiring way, it works in conjunction with other organs to support life and new growth.

So I bless my heart and give thanks to God for its healthy, strong beat. I envision it as strong and steady, yet filled to overflowing with divine love.

As vital as my heart is to my physical health and well-being, it is even more important to my spiritual life and growth. My heart is a soul center of love and peace and joy, for through my heartfelt acts of kindness, I share God's love with others.

It is amazing! The more love and joy I pour forth from my heart, the more I use it as an instrument of God's love and the healthier I feel in mind and body!

> **"God is the strength of my heart and my portion forever."**
> **—Psalm 73:26**

Day 218

—◆—

Thank You, God, for creating such diversity in the world.

DIVERSITY It has been said that no two snowflakes are alike, and if I were to take a random sampling of them, I would indeed notice the variations in size and shape—each one intricately beautiful and unique.

As one of God's children, I, too, am unique. At times, I may wish others were more like me and would some-how come around to my way of thinking, but the world would be rather humdrum if all people looked, acted, and thought alike.

Part of the beauty and wonder of life is the diversity that individual uniqueness nourishes, so rather than resist those differences in other people, I understand and give thanks that each person is a unique individual created by God.

Thank You, God, for creating such diversity in the world. Thank You for each unique creation, whether snowflake or individual.

"For we are what he has made us."—Ephesians 2:10

DAILY WORD

Day 219

—◆—

*I am prosperous, for God blesses me—
heart and soul!*

BLESSINGS Prosperity is so much more than having enough money to pay bills and buy new things. True prosperity is an abundance of all kinds of blessings: loving friends, harmonious relationships, true happiness, and inner peace.

I may have a job to earn money or provide some service that someone is willing to pay for, but what can I do to earn happiness, joy, and peace? The good news is that I do not have to earn these blessings! God provides for my prosperity so that I am blessed by spiritually enriched living!

As I work with God, I open myself to a whole world of abundance. God already knows my needs and the desires of my heart. In my partnership with God, I am assured of receiving whatever blesses my heart and soul.

**"God is able to provide you with every
blessing in abundance."
—2 Corinthians 9:8**

Day 220

—◆—

Using my imagination, I help create a world of harmony.

IMAGINATION

It is true—my thoughts help create my reality, so I use my thoughts in a positive way: I let my imagination create a vision of world harmony.

I begin that vision with me as an ambassador of peace and let this dream become my reality. I greet others with a smile and a kind word, silently blessing them on their way.

I see every family member, friend, and co-worker peace-filled and free. I trust God to show them their own paths and to show them how to express their uniqueness without fear of rejection.

Now I expand my vision to include the entire planet. I bless the people and the situations of each country and imagine the world as God created it to be—filled with love and harmony.

> "Now to him who . . .
> is able to accomplish abundantly far more
> than all we can ask or imagine, to him be glory."
> —Ephesians 3:20–21

Day 221

—◆—

I am loved and loving!

LOVE

When someone says, "I love you," I feel good—secure and at peace. And my response may be, "I love you, too!"

Yet God's love *for* me brings out an even greater response *from* me. Divine love encourages me to do and be my best. Knowing that God loves me gives me reason to rejoice, because I know I am loved unconditionally! With God, I know that I am important, that I have something to contribute to the world.

God is always with me, so God's love is always with me, too, and nothing can make God love me less. Nothing—absolutely nothing—can keep God's love from me. So I do not let anything keep me from expressing God's love to others. I am loving, and my life is filled with joy!

"For I am convinced that neither death, nor life, nor angels, nor rulers . . . nor anything else in all creation, will be able to separate us from the love of God."
—Romans 8:38–39

Day 222

—◆—

With every prayer, I wish you love.

PRAYER FOR A LOVED ONE

My greatest wish for you comes from a desire for your well-being. And that wish is that you experience love in all that you do—not just any love but the unconditional, healing, strengthening love of God.

With every thought of you and prayer for you, I wish you love. Love is the strength of your convictions, the tenderness of your attitude, and the wisdom of your decisions.

Love goes with you where I am unable to go, gently guiding you on unfamiliar pathways. Love is your assurance that you can make it through any challenge and come through whole and free and well.

Yes, I wish you love. Love comforts, assures, and enlivens you, for love is the spirit of God living in and through you and reaching out from me to you.

**"If you abide in me, and my words abide in you, ask for whatever you wish, and it will be done for you."
—John 15:7**

Day 223

—◆—

My commitment is to living
a God-centered life.

COMMITMENT TO GOD
God, as I begin this day, I give thanks for Your presence. In all matters, I remain centered on Your power and open to Your guidance. Guide me, teach me, love me, for I am Your child and student—ready, willing, and able to carry on Your work of kindness and goodwill to all.

Your love and support are all that I need to experience true happiness, so I make a commitment to living my life from Your spirit within me. You are my world, my sustenance, my very reason for being, and I live my life as You guide me to live it.

You are my best friend, and for this, I am truly grateful. As my humble gift to you, I joyfully dedicate and commit myself to leading a God-centered life.

Thank You, God, for loving me, guiding me, and always being present in my life.

> "Do not lag in zeal, be ardent in spirit,
> serve the Lord."
> —Romans 12:11

Day 224

—◆—

*I am open to God's way, which is
always the best way.*

A BETTER WAY

One of the hardest lessons in life is that "my way" is not always the best way! So if I have a decision to make or I am looking for a new idea, I know to remain open-minded always. God will show me the better way.

How can I know if I am doing what God wants me to do? I turn to God in prayer, ask for guidance, and then listen. In the quiet of prayer, God speaks to me with an idea or a feeling that comforts and strengthens me.

I draw upon God's strength when I am dealing with others and when I am alone. It does not matter how serious or trivial the current situation may seem; I can always rely on God and know that what happens will be in my best interest.

Because I am open to God's way, I discover the best way.

> "Strive for the greater gifts. And I will show you
> a still more excellent way."
> —1 Corinthians 12:31

Day 225

—◆—

I care for loved ones, knowing that God
prepares me to give the best care.

I CARE

Almost in the same thought, I may be questioning if what I am doing for someone is enough or if it is too much. I understand that sometimes a caring attitude fuels an enthusiasm that may make it seem as if I am taking over for people rather than helping them out.

Yet I do care and want to help. So I take it person by person, situation by situation. For some, I need only offer a steady hand they can hold on to when the going gets rough. For others, I may be guided to tend to their every need in the short term or in the long term. So I call on God for the understanding, strength, and patience to give them the best possible care.

And when I am separated from loved ones, I know that I can make a positive difference in their lives through my prayers for them.

> "He went to him and bandaged his wounds. . . .
> And took care of him."
> —Luke 10:34

Day 226

—◆—

With confidence and courage,
I proclaim: With God, I can!

WITH GOD, I CAN
Most children have been read to and taught from stories of courage about people who overcame great odds and went on to victory. Even today these stories can evoke feelings of courage and confidence from people of all ages.

So today, I mentally stand tall and proudly declare: *With God, I can!* I use these simple yet powerful words as a dynamic, daily affirmation which reminds me that with a little common sense and a lot of faith in the power of God, I can do anything. I can be strong! I can do what needs to be done! I can be all that I want to be and even more! I can! I can!

I am only limited by how far my thoughts can take me, and when I connect with the all-powerful mind of God, I am unlimited. *I can!*

"Did I not tell you that if you believed, you would see the glory of God?"
—John 11:40

Day 227

—◆—

*God's grace strengthens and
restores me.*

**DIVINE
GRACE**

How empowering it is to know that
I do not need to depend on someone
or depend on something to give me
strength! Through God's grace, I have
all that I need to meet and overcome every challenge.

So if I feel that I have been treated unfairly, I release
the outworking of the situation to God. As I do, I let go
any discomfort over the situation and know that divine
love and grace will bring about the right outcome for
me and for everyone else. *Divine* justice and harmony
always prevail.

No matter what is happening in my life, I know that
the help and support I need will always be there for me.
This is divine grace in action. I trust God and let divine
grace bring me order and peace of mind.

God's grace is constantly strengthening and
restoring me.

**"The God of all grace . . . will himself restore,
support, strengthen, and establish you."
—1 Peter 5:10**

Day 228

In this very moment, I am living in the presence of God.

HOLY GROUND

Angels played an important part in Bible stories, for they were God's messengers of inspiration.

Like angels, divine ideas fill my mind and convey to me the good news: The spirit of God is reborn in me now!

Every day is a new beginning; each moment is a new opportunity to experience God's presence in my life. When I pray, I become aware that God is the very life within me. I am opening my mind and heart to divine ideas that enrich my life.

Wherever I am right now, I am living in the presence of God. I am open to divine inspiration, and as I prepare to receive it, I am filled with the joy of Spirit.

Like the angels in the Bible, I rejoice, for truly I am on holy ground.

> "The angel replied, 'I am Gabriel. I stand in the presence of God, and I have been sent to speak to you and to bring you this good news.'"
> —Luke 1:19

Day 229

—◆—

*Thank You, God, for pouring out
blessing upon blessing!*

**I Am
Thankful!**

Today I can give thanks for so
much—even if I think I have little to be
thankful for!

I begin by giving thanks for God's
spirit within me. When I start with God, I find that I
have so much to be thankful for. Then I don't concentrate on what I lack; instead, I concentrate on what I
have and the potential for even more of God's blessings.

The moment I fully know that God is the source of
all that blesses me, I understand that a sunrise or a
sunset, gentle rain or blooming flowers may seem
amazing yet are everyday happenings of beauty and
wonder that bless me and others.

When I start giving thanks, my thanksgiving comes
full circle and includes the blessings God pours out to
me, my family, my friends, and people of the whole
world every day.

> **"Rejoice always, pray without ceasing, give
> thanks in all circumstances."**
> **—1 Thessalonians 5:16–18**

Day 230

I step forth in faith!

STEP FORTH   Just for a moment I imagine the surge of relief and faith felt by those who were there to witness Lazarus as he stepped forth *alive* from the tomb. What if I had been there when Jesus called out to Lazarus? Would I have immediately believed Jesus? Would I have felt exhilaration, anticipation, expectation? Or would such an occurrence have been far removed from anything that I could ever have imagined?

When Lazarus did step forth from the tomb, even those who had doubted immediately believed. Today I can still learn the valuable lesson that those who bore witness to this event learned: Through the power of the indwelling Spirit, all things are possible—if I believe.

"The time is fulfilled, and the kingdom of God has come near . . . believe in the good news."
—Mark 1:15

Day 231

—◆—

Letting go and letting God opens a whole new life for me.

NEW LIFE Certainly, Jesus was a magnificent example of absolute faith in God. Facing death, Jesus affirmed: "Not my will but yours be done." And out of that faith came the resurrection. Letting go and letting God, Jesus overcame death and all in the universe that would try to limit Him.

And so it is with me. I am following in the footsteps of Jesus when I let go and let God. Then I am not only learning or reading about Jesus, I am living the principles that He applied in His own life.

Sometimes I may have to reach to the core of my being for the strength and wisdom to get through a challenge, but the spirit of God is at that core.

Letting go and letting God opens a whole new world, a whole new life, a whole new *me*—all of which continue to unfold with each new day.

"Not my will but yours be done."
—Luke 22:42

Day 232

—◆—

I take a quantum leap in
spiritual awareness.

TRANSFORMA-
TION

My mind is set, my mental and
physical faculties are in sync with my
faith and with my prayers, and the spirit
of God within me is taking charge. With
each thought, word, and action, I let the spirit of God
shine through me as love and understanding.

I feel a tremendous strength building within me.
With each passing moment, I am guided to release
more and more of my limitations until there can be no
more. Slowly but surely, I am learning to recognize my
divine potential. As I make a personal commitment to
live from the spirit of God within me, I have made a
quantum leap in spiritual awareness.

I am in transition, making a dynamic move forward
into the spiritual dimension. The spirit of God is within
me, and I am becoming more and more aware of the
spiritual person I was created to be.

"Know that I am with you."
—Genesis 28:15

Day 233

—◆—

My faith in God is a confidence builder.

CONFIDENCE BUILDER

When a baby bird is ready to leave the nest and fly, it may hesitate for a few seconds before taking the plunge into the air. As the fledgling teeters precariously on the edge, the parents, although nearby, stay back. They follow their instinct and allow the baby to do what needs to be done by it to better its own life.

As a child of God, I also have the faith and strength of purpose to do those things that need to be done by me. I can explore the unknown and accept all that life has to offer me.

And if loved ones or friends are going through changes, I have the strength to let them do what they need to do—all the time offering support and encouragement. With faith that God is always in charge, I move into the unknown with assurance and confidence.

"Commit your way to the Lord."
—Psalm 37:5

Day 234

——◆——

My first commitment is to love God, which is a willingness to love all.

COMMITMENT TO LOVE

Despite what I might have associated with the word *commitment* in the past, I now know that it can be the most freeing, fulfilling activity of mind and heart.

This is true because my first commitment is to love God. Because I love God, I love all that God has created. I love my family, my co-workers, and my friends just as I love myself.

Do I love myself? I do when I love God, when I love the presence of God, the spirit of the divinity that is within me. This is the divine self within me and all the people in my life. The love *of* God and love *for* God within me create an environment of acceptance. I love because it is my nature to love. A commitment to love God is a resolution to love all that God has created.

"You shall love the Lord your God with all your heart, and with all your soul, and with all your mind."
—Matthew 22:37

Day 235

——◆——

God is with me always.

WITHIN ME ALWAYS
When I truly listen, can I hear God around me? When I really look, do I see the divine Presence in every living thing in my world? When I am absolutely still, can I feel God within and around me? *Yes,* God is everywhere!

The voice of God is carried as a whisper on the wind, as the comforting sound of a loved one, as the peaceful reassurance I hear during times of prayer. If I need to be at peace, I can be, for God is here with me to calm and assure me.

God is everywhere—in every person, in every star, in every tree, in every animal as the one Power and Presence that created all.

God is within me—ready to comfort and reassure me. I need not ever feel alone in any situation, because God is with me—always.

"Go in peace. The mission you are on is under the eye of the Lord."
—Judges 18:6

Day 236

—◆—

I live my life centered in the harmony of God.

ONE PEOPLE

One of the most beautiful stories of acceptance, love, and harmony between people is about a mother and her daughter-in-law.

Naomi and Ruth—both widowed and from different lands, raised in different religions and cultures—lived together in the love and harmony of God.

Just another story? No, it is also a way of life, a way of living in harmony with people who seem different at least on the outside. When labels of differences are peeled away, as Naomi and Ruth did, people everywhere discover that truly there is one people, created by one God.

The God-life present in each person radiates out to create an atmosphere of harmony within families and the world.

> **"Your people shall be my people,**
> **and your God my God."**
> **—Ruth 1:16**

Day 237

—◆—

I am a child of God, living and learning in a world of great possibilities.

CHILD OF GOD

Sometimes life may seem like a giant puzzle, and I am not sure where I fit into the overall picture. Maybe I am feeling confused because I have not yet realized who I am.

I am a child of God, created by God and created to express spiritual attributes. I share a divine heritage with everyone I meet, and this awareness creates an atmosphere of goodwill in which I can grow and learn and achieve.

Because I am a child of God, living and learning in a world of great possibilities, there is always hope—hope for what I desire to accomplish and hope for what I believe I can and will do.

So whatever it is that I set out to do, I do it with the understanding that I am God's child. I know that I fit in and feel right at home with the rest of God's family.

"It is that very Spirit bearing witness with our spirit that we are children of God."
—Romans 8:16

Day 238

—◆—

God is my full-time partner and guide.

DIVINE PARTNER — Why is it that when I have prayed about a situation, received guidance, and feel that it is right, I still may hesitate to follow through with some action?

Saying yes to a commitment, a relationship, a goal, or a new way of life is just the beginning. Then comes the day-to-day work and dedication to it.

Yet one thing I know through it all: God is my full-time partner and guide. Just as surely as I have received the guidance to make a decision, I will also be continually guided in giving what I have to give, in doing what I have to do to fulfill it.

God has brought me this far and will be with me always. When I really know that this is true, I have all the courage and confidence I will ever need.

> **"You hold my right hand.**
> **You guide me with your counsel."**
> **—Psalm 73:23–24**

Day 239

—◆—

My words are treasures of the heart, for they speak of harmony and love.

TREASURED WORDS

Throughout His ministry, Jesus demonstrated the amazing power of the spoken word. He spoke with faith and authority, with compassion and belief, saying, "Out of the abundance of the heart the mouth speaks."

Today and every day, I follow Jesus' example and speak words of power and wisdom. I rely on God to guide me, so I know that my words will be loving and kind, that they will promote harmony in my own world and throughout the planet.

I want every word that comes out of my mouth to be a message of goodwill from God. God speaks through me to proclaim the good news: Great joy is available to all of us when we recognize and give thanks for the treasure we have to share.

"Out of the abundance of the heart the mouth speaks. The good person brings good things out of a good treasure."
—Matthew 12:34–35

Day 240

—◆—

*Prayer is the master key to
well-being.*

**MASTER
KEY**

I know that it is important for me to take good care of myself, especially when others rely on me to be there for them. So I try to get plenty of rest, eat right, and exercise regularly. But even more important is the time I spend with God in prayer.

Prayer is the key to my total well-being. It keeps me focused on what is important—God and my own spirituality. As I develop and maintain my relationship with God, I am nourished and sustained in spirit, mind, and body.

There is no feeling quite like the one I experience when I know I am cared for and loved by God. I share this feeling with others by holding them in prayer and knowing that God is with them every step of their way.

"God is able to provide you with every blessing
in abundance, so that by always having enough of
everything, you may share abundantly in every
good work."
—2 Corinthians 9:8

Day 241

—◆—

I'm ready for a miracle!

READY FOR A MIRACLE   Do I ever stop what I am doing just to take in the miracles that are happening all around and within me? From the blossoming of flowers to the wonder of new life to the beating of my own heart, miracles are taking place. Am I ready for more?

How about the miracle that is me? I am a unique and important creation of God—living proof that miracles exist. Every part of me was made especially *for* me—my inquisitive mind, my loving heart, my divinely inspired soul. With every breath I take, I am experiencing the miracle of life—the miracle of God moving in me and out from me into my life.

I am ready for a miracle! So I open my mind and my heart to God, and I let the wonder of the Divine be expressed in what I think, feel, say, and do.

> **"Strive for the greater gifts. And I will show you a still more excellent way."**
> **—1 Corinthians 12:31**

Day 242

—◆—

*I remain ever one in spirit
with God and with my loved ones.*

TREASURES OF THE HEART
Some of my greatest treasures are keepsakes that remind me of my loved ones. Looking at photographs, letters, and cards stirs up memories of people who are dear to my heart.

The images of loved ones in photographs remain forever young, although the people I love and cherish may have aged and even passed away. The real truth about these people, about all people, cannot be captured by a camera.

We are *all* forever young in spirit! As spiritual beings, we do take on physical form. Although the physical form is changeable, spirit is eternal. We are eternally alive in spirit!

More than memories connect me with my loved ones. I remain forever one in spirit with God and with my loved ones.

"I am with you always."
—Matthew 28:20

Day 243

—◆—

*My thoughts of others are God-centered
thoughts of love and acceptance.*

**LOVING
THOUGHTS**
I know that my thoughts help create
my experiences. Thinking positive
thoughts about myself helps me to do
and be my best always.

The same is true of my relationships. If I am thinking
the best about my family and friends, I bring the best to
my relationships with them.

The very best thoughts I can think are God-centered
thoughts of love, acceptance, and forgiveness. So I
don't think less of friends and loved ones than what
is true about them: They are children of God who
deserve to be thought of with true, honorable, just,
and positive thoughts.

My loving, patient thoughts create loving, long-
lasting relationships.

"Finally, beloved, whatever is true, whatever is
honorable, whatever is just, whatever is pure,
whatever is pleasing, whatever is commendable . . .
think about these things."
—Philippians 4:8

Day 244

I behold the spirit of God in myself and in others.

LOOK AGAIN   When I look in a mirror, whom do I see? Do I see the same person I have been looking at for years? Same eyes, same nose, same mouth—all the features I have grown accustomed to and probably take for granted.

Now I look again, but with spiritual vision that sees beyond physical features to the real me that lies within. Whom do I see now? If I am really looking past appearances, I will discover me, a dynamic, loving person who is unique and wonderful in my own special way.

I look at the people around me and discover the beauty and wonder of God's spirit within them! Now I am so glad I took another look!

"For now we see in a mirror, dimly, but then we will see face to face. Now I know only in part; then I will know fully, even as I have been fully known."
—1 Corinthians 13:12

Day 245

God has given me all this—and more!

SOMETHING MORE

Do I feel as if there is something better than what I am now experiencing waiting for me just around the corner?

Or maybe I feel an urgency to discover something more that is just beyond my grasp. I am right; there is more! Even with all that I now have and hope to have, God has something more for me!

It is God's good pleasure to give me the kingdom, which includes health, inner peace, and unlimited abundance! So whether I feel that there is more waiting for me in a certain career or in a more fulfilling relationship, I know that God is always ready to give me more peace, happiness, and soul satisfaction.

> "Is not life more than food, and the body more than clothing? Look at the birds of the air; they neither sow nor reap nor gather into barns, and yet your heavenly Father feeds them. Are you not of more value than they?"
> —Matthew 6:25–26

Day 246

---◆---

*In sweet surrender to God, I clear
my mind and refresh my soul.*

**RELEASE
IT**

Is there a heaviness of heart that I
carry around with me? Perhaps something happened to me or to a loved
one, and I just cannot get over the hurt
of it.

Yet in order to live my life, I need to get far enough
away from that incident so that I do not keep reliving
the hurt. How do I do this? I release it not in anger, but
in a sweet surrender to God. In sweet surrender, I clear
my mind and refresh my soul.

I am not the condition that happened to me. I am a
beloved creation of God. Whenever harsh memories
come to mind, I release them and begin to know that I
can overcome them.

I do not deny that something happened; I just deny
that it has the power to control me and my life. In
sweet surrender to God, I will know how it is to be
completely alive and whole.

"You will find rest for your souls."
—Matthew 11:29

Day 247

——◆——

My heart sings with joy!

HEART OF JOY

When I think about the people and events that have blessed me, my heart sings with joy! I am a remarkable creation of a loving God, surrounded by life and abundance. I am so glad to be alive!

Each person I know fills a special role in my life story! The love and happiness I feel when I am with them remind me of the deep wellspring of joy within. I know that this joy comes from God, for God is the source of all the joy in the universe.

As I recognize and give thanks for all the blessings in life, I feel in awe of the wonder that God is. Knowing that I am an important part of God's overall plan, I let my joy and appreciation come forth freely.

> "For you shall go out in joy,
> and be led back in peace;
> the mountains and the hills before you
> shall burst into song."
> —Isaiah 55:12

Day 248

—◆—

God's grace is active in my life.

GIFT OF GRACE

When I think of the wonder of God's grace, I feel a surge of love and appreciation moving through me. Oh what gifts God has given to the world!

One gift that comes to mind is the magnificent planet earth. In my own home and community, there are cherished family and friends who are examples of God's grace in action. In fact, every breath I take is a gift from God.

Grace gives me all the joy, peace, and love I can fill myself with and the abundant *more* that is left over. Grace is the assurance that no matter what I do, God is there for me, accepting me and loving me. Knowing that God's grace is active in my life, I can meet any situation with faith. I know without a doubt that God's grace is active in my life and is a gift of love that keeps on giving.

> **"By the grace of God I am what I am,
> and his grace toward me has not been in vain."
> —1 Corinthians 15:10**

Day 249

—◆—

Thank God for loved ones!

FOR MY LOVED ONES God, I know that one of the most loving things I can do for others is to pray for them. So today and every day, I give thanks to You for my loved ones, for the blessings they have been and continue to be, for the joy and happiness I receive just thinking about them.

God, when You created my loved ones, You created people of pure love and joy. I am blessed by the opportunity to know them. It is an honor and a blessing to share my life with them.

And, God, I thank You for the tender care only You can give to those who are so precious to me. No matter how far away they may be from me, I feel so much peace in knowing that You are always with them, providing for their safety and well-being.

Thank You, thank You, God!

> **"When I remember you in my prayers,
> I always thank my God."**
> **—Philemon 1:4**

Day 250

—◆—

In tune with my divine nature, I fulfill my divine potential.

DIVINE POTENTIAL
If someday I am watching a young downy swan that is learning to walk, would I be able to see past its stumbling, awkward appearance to what it will be one day? Could I envision the graceful swan that will soon emerge as one of nature's most beautiful sights?

If I am beginning my spiritual walk, I may appear awkward to others, and I may even stumble about. But when the time comes that I am aware of my oneness with God, that I am completely in tune with my divine nature and express pure love and peace, I, too, will become as graceful and spectacular as that swan.

I owe it to myself and to God not to give up on the wonderful, divine potential that I am capable of fulfilling.

"Be transformed by the renewing of your minds,
so that you may discern . . . what is good and
acceptable and perfect."
—Romans 12:2

Day 251

—◆—

I free my thoughts and prepare the way for positive living.

PREPARATION

If I were planning a flower garden of color, texture, and form, my first step would be to prepare the ground for planting. So I would pull up any weeds that might later interfere with the growth of the flowers, knowing that weeding only one time will not be enough. To ensure the growth of my flowers, I weed my garden regularly.

The same holds true in the garden of my soul where thoughts and faith come together to form a spirituality that nourishes and sustains me. If I continue to weed my mind of hurt feelings and angry thoughts, then I am clearing the way for positive images to grow and flourish.

It is true—love and understanding will come forth as I free my thoughts and prepare the way for positive living.

> "Keep your heart with all vigilance,
> for from it flow the springs of life."
> —Proverbs 4:23

Day 252

—◆—

I am living the spiritual freedom that God created me to live.

**SONG
OF
FREEDOM**

I hear a gentle urging to know and live my freedom now. It begins as a whisper of a song, "Live the spiritual freedom that God created you to live."

As I let this message of freedom play in my heart and mind, I cannot forget its divine melody. It is a prayer of faith which reminds me that no negative habit or tendency can come between me and the quality of life I want to experience.

I am living the spiritual freedom that God created me to live. The power of God's spirit within me is far greater than any habit. I have strength of spirit that can overcome any problem or concern.

Each time I think of or pray for those who are seeking to break away from limitations, I know the truth for them; they, too, can live their spiritual freedom now!

**"For you were called to freedom,
brothers and sisters."
—Galatians 5:13**

Day 253

—◆—

God blesses me with life.

BLESSING OF LIFE God has given me a wondrous gift—the gift of life—and I joyously accept it.

As I breathe in, the breath of God fills my lungs, and I receive divine strength. Every cell and every muscle of my body reverberates with this strength from God.

The love of God fills my heart. I express love and understanding to those around me. I live by the Golden Rule and treat others as I would like them to treat me.

The peace of God fills my mind. I bask in the glow of divine light and love, and I am able to relax, for God is in charge. I am filled with an everlasting peace that comes from knowing pure joy and contentment.

God is eternal, and because the spirit of God fills my mind, heart, and body, I am forever one with all that is divine. God blesses me with life.

"My soul is satisfied as with a rich feast."
—Psalm 63:5

Day 254

—◆—

I am a spiritual being on a divine journey.

BREAK THROUGH

Right now I know that I am standing on the threshold of a breakthrough—a spiritual journey that will take me further along in my growth than I could ever possibly imagine.

This is a journey on which I will be filled with a peace that far surpasses anything I have ever experienced, and I begin it by knowing and living the truth of my divine potential.

I am on a journey of positive thinking, praying, and living. If ever I find myself falling into a rut of negative thinking, I don't break down—I break through! I break through the barriers of those negative thoughts and that less-than-positive attitude. I break through and discover that I am a spiritual being on a divine journey.

"I am about to do a new thing;
now it springs forth, do you not perceive it?"
—Isaiah 43:19

Day 255

—◆—

I let go and let God, opening the way for a divine solution.

LET GO, LET GOD

When I have done all that I humanly can do to make something work but it does not, it is time to take a "breather" and get away from the situation. Later, I will be able to give it a fresh look.

There is something even more helpful I can do when I seem stuck in a problem. I can let go and let God. Letting go and letting God works because it causes me to think of God first, not the various experiences I am going through. I am being responsible when I let go because I know that I am letting God take charge.

When I let go, I am giving up the tendency to think that I must come up with the perfect answer to every problem. When I let God, I am opening up the way for a divine solution. God's way can never fail, because it is the way of truth and love.

> "No one can do these signs that you do apart
> from the presence of God."
> —John 3:2

Day 256

—◆—

My search is over—I have found God.

MY SEARCH How many times have I lost something and searched frantically for it, only to discover that it was right under my nose the whole time? I was so intent on finding what I had lost that I looked right past it.

Something similar may happen in my search for truth and for the answer to the age-old question, "Who am I?" The answer is so close to me that I might be overlooking it—the answer is God in me.

So I take a look at myself. Do I see the light of God shining forth from my eyes? Ah, yes, there it is! In that light I see that I am a beloved child of God, made in the divine image. God created me to express spirituality. If I have been looking here and there to become more spiritual, my search is over. The spirit of God is and always has been within me.

"When you search for me, you will find me."
—Jeremiah 29:13

Day 257

—◆—

Divine power heals and
rejuvenates me.

DIVINE
POWER
HEALS

My body is in a continuous state of change because every cell is constantly being rejuvenated.

There is always new life within me. My body is in a perpetual state of renewal, and even though I may look the same day after day, I am not. From the inside out, I am being made fresh and new.

The same divine power that guides the cells in my body to rejuvenate themselves has influence over every aspect of my well-being. So if I am feeling less than well and whole, I remember what is right with me rather than getting caught up in thoughts of what is wrong.

What is right is that God is renewing me. Divine life and activity are constant, restoring me to health and keeping me healthy.

> **"Your light shall break forth like the dawn,**
> **and your healing shall spring up quickly."**
> **—Isaiah 58:8**

Day 258

—◆—

I infuse my relationships with love and harmony.

UNIVERSAL SPIRITUALITY What a great example of living in love and harmony Jesus gave to the world with His simple request for a drink of water. Jews and Samaritans were divided by great differences, yet Jesus was able to turn aside differences and bring out the truth of universal spirituality when He spoke to and taught a Samaritan woman at the well.

In everyday living, I, too, have many opportunities to infuse my relationships and my interactions with others with harmony. As I do, I nourish myself and my relationships by bringing to light my own spirituality and that of others.

The spirit of God is within us all and unites us in love and harmony. I can never meet a person who does not have the spirit of God within, so I help each person discover inner harmony and express it.

> "Those who drink of the water that I will give them will never be thirsty."
> —John 4:14

DAILY WORD

Day 259

—◆—

I am a beloved child of God.

SPIRITUAL IDENTITY The ending of a relationship or a job can cause me to question myself and what it is that I want out of life. Such questioning may not always be a negative thing. It can help me get my life back together, but it will do so only if I let it build me up, not tear me down.

I have within me the source of all that I need to be happy and successful—the loving spirit of God. So I make sure that I am relying on my inner guide—not outer appearances—when I make decisions that will have a major impact on my life. I go about relying on God when I seek divine guidance in prayer.

In the quiet of prayer I am assured: "You are my . . . Beloved; with you I am well-pleased." I know without a doubt that I have God's love and support, so how can I *not* succeed?

"With you I am well-pleased."
—Mark 1:11

Day 260

—◆—

*New doors to opportunity
open before me.*

Toddlers achieve a milestone in their young lives when they take their first step. Yet what may seem to be one small step for these children is so much more. It is the beginning of a wonderful journey.

With the simple act of putting one foot in front of the other, children are displaying amazing courage. They are moving ahead, and doorways to new opportunities and new adventures are opening wide.

I, too, can open new doorways by having the courage to follow God's guidance and by doing what I need to do to better myself. I won't hold myself back with negative habits or thoughts. With God's help and encouragement, I can step out in faith and change my life forever.

With God's help, new doors to opportunity open before me.

**"If you have faith the size of a mustard seed . . .
nothing will be impossible for you."
—Matthew 17:20**

Day 261

*I give my best and expect the best
from others.*

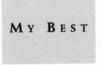

MY BEST

My plan for today is to give my best and to expect the best from others. And what makes this plan such a workable one is that the very best—the divine self—is always within everyone and ready to respond through everyone.

The divine self within me is kind, loving, and caring. So as I speak to people, I use words of love, comfort, and support. I give voice to a language of the soul that encourages a like response from others.

Then I am willing to go the extra mile by doing more. I can be patient with the adult who is full of impatience, and I can be understanding with the child who feels misunderstood.

When I both give and expect the best, the very least that can happen is that I bring out the best in me and others.

> "Therefore I do my best always to have a clear
> conscience toward God and all people."
> —Acts 24:16

Day 262

—◆—

*I live from the peace of God
within me.*

**LIVING IN
PEACE**

Sometimes there is an ache within me that is not a physical pain, but a longing for relief of heart and mind. Whenever this happens, I know that this is a desire for peace at the deepest level of my soul.

And I know there is relief, there is hope, for God has created me with a reservoir of inner peace. It is up to me to release the peace of God within me so that it can flow through me, so that it can wash away anxiety and fear.

I already own all the peace I could ever desire, and I claim it now. Even when I am in the middle of a dilemma, I am serene. Even if there seems to be no way out of or around a problem, I know that there is, and I am peaceful. As I let the peace of God rise up within me, I am uplifted in thought, in spirit, and in expectations.

**"May the God of hope fill you with all joy and
peace in believing."
—Romans 15:13**

Day 263

—◆—

I am healthy and whole—one of God's creations of energy and life.

PICTURE OF HEALTH

I picture for a moment how I would feel if I were the healthiest I have ever been or ever hoped to be. Now I hold that picture in mind. I envision myself full of life, with every cell in my body celebrating life.

What I am picturing is true, for I was created for life—for ever-renewing life. God created me with life and intelligence in every cell of my body.

Now I picture myself accomplishing my heart's desire—learning a new skill, overcoming a fear. This is a true picture also, for God created me to express life in wonderful ways. So as I imagine all I can do, I am preparing for it.

I am doing more than idle daydreaming. I am painting a true picture of me as one of God's creations of energy and life.

"The eye is the lamp of the body. So, if your eye is healthy, your whole body will be full of light."
—Matthew 6:22

Day 264

—◆—

I am inspired by my faith in God!

CORNER-STONE OF FAITH

Faith in God is a cornerstone on which I build my life. Yet when I first come up against a challenge or when one seems to reach unmanageable proportions, I may be so focused on the challenge that I forget how faith-filled I am.

Right where I am—even in the middle of a crisis—all the positive prayers and thoughts and actions from the past are a lifeline in awareness to divine inner power. I discover that I am stronger and wiser than I ever before realized I could be.

It is true: God never gives up on me, even when I am ready to give up on myself. Faith rushes in when I leave the door to my heart and mind open even a tiny crack. Faith creates an atmosphere of hope that draws to me the right people, jobs, ideas, and whatever else I need.

> **"Now faith is the assurance of things hoped for,**
> **the conviction of things not seen."**
> **—Hebrews 11:1**

Day 265

—◆—

God created me with
great possibilities.

GREAT POSSIBILITIES
When a spacecraft re-enters the atmosphere on its return trip to earth, there is only a narrow window of space through which it can safely pass. There is one chance to hit the mark or the ship will either be hurled back into space or completely destroyed upon re-entry.

And maybe something in my life seems to be a once-in-a-lifetime opportunity—the result of luck or chance. But I know that with God, nothing is left to chance. Through the spirit of God within me, I have been given all that I will ever need to be successful throughout my life.

God loves me with an everlasting love, and God created me for many great possibilities. Whatever plans I have for this day, I know that nothing happens by chance, that God is guiding me down a path that will lead to true joy and lasting peace.

"I am with you always."
—Matthew 28:20

Day 266

—◆—

God is my source of joy and gladness.

JOY

There is a quiet, sacred joy in knowing that I am one with the presence of God within me and within the universe.

Once I know of my oneness with my Creator, I experience a gladness that defies definition. This is a joy that reaches to the depths of my soul, soothing, healing, and refreshing me.

As I allow that joy to build within me, I will soon find that it begins to spill over into all that I say and do. I take such delight in life—in all it has to offer me and in all that I have to offer life.

There is great joy in knowing God, in knowing that God is always with me. Although I find joy in experiences, people, and things, I no longer look to them as my source. God is my joy.

"I have said these things to you so that my joy may be in you, and that your joy may be complete."
—John 15:11

Day 267

—◆—

*The spirit of God enlivens me, and I am
spiritually enriched.*

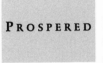

PROSPERED God, I was thinking about how
prosperous I would feel if I had
absolutely no concerns about money
or material things.

Then I thought how such a feeling about things
would wane in comparison with how spiritually rich I
feel each time I take the time to talk with You, each time
I become still and know that Your spirit lives within me.

I feel prosperous because I feel Your presence within
me. I am prosperous because Your spirit enlivens me,
Your wisdom guides me, and Your love created me.
There is no amount of money that can buy the life that
You have already given me, no material thing that is as
precious as Your loving, comforting presence.

**"The spirit of God has made me,
and the breath of the Almighty gives me life."
—Job 33:4**

Day 268

—◆—

*My greatest success is in realizing my
own sacredness.*

SACREDNESS

Being successful means more—so
much more—to me than being at the
top in the business field or in financial
circles. That rush of feeling successful
comes from a genuine, heartfelt belief in and an understanding of my own sacredness.

Giving 100 percent of myself means that I allow the
spirit of God to guide me in important as well as everyday matters. Then I will succeed at being the best I can
be. The rewards of having given something as valuable
as love and kindness leave me feeling good about
myself and what I have done.

God has provided me with whatever it takes to be
successful in whatever I do. Now it is up to me to use
those qualities of Spirit that are mine to use, to give
each endeavor my all. Yet all the while, I know my
greatest success is in realizing my own sacredness.

**"You will say to this mountain, 'Move from here
to there,' and it will move."
—Matthew 17:20**

Day 269

—◆—

Children, you are safe and secure in God's loving presence.

BLESS THE CHILDREN
I may feel anxious about my children when they are away from me, because I cannot see them or touch them to reassure myself that they are okay. But I can be assured that even when *I* cannot see them or be with them, God is.

We are all God's children, and from the tiniest infant to the most mature adult, we are enfolded in God's loving presence. Wherever we go and whatever we do, God's loving presence is with us.

So I teach my children to have good judgment, but I also show them by example what it is to lead a prayerful, faith-filled life. I know this is true for me and my loved ones: God goes with us wherever we go, and in God's presence, we are secure.

"You will have confidence, because there is hope; you will be protected and take your rest in safety."
—Job 11:18

Day 270

—◆—

God's love and peace flow through me to bless others.

GOD'S HANDS

God, my hands are Your hands, so I give thanks for them and ask for Your guidance in using them to bless others.

Fill my hands with Your love, and use them to bring comfort where there is pain, encouragement where there is despair.

Guide my hands and fill them with Your strength so that I might help the ones who need to be uplifted.

Empower my hands with the skill they need to accomplish Your mighty works. Your work in my hands is a true labor of love, and I am grateful for every opportunity to work with You to bring peace and joy to others.

Bless my hands and extend Your love through them, making them an instrument of Your peace. As Your love flows through me and reaches out to others, I am blessed and filled with joy.

"What deeds of power are being done by his hands!"
—Mark 6:2

Day 271

—◆—

I live in the now—a time of spiritual growth and discovery.

LIVING NOW   Although I may have plans for the future—for my special dreams and goals—I realize that right now, this very moment, is the time frame in which I live.

How important it is to live each day, each moment knowing I am one with God and one with the spirit of God within others. This understanding satisfies a deep longing of my soul. I am so satisfied that I am not continually wanting more things or rushing to complete some project.

I am living in the now, affirming that each moment I can begin anew. If I was disappointed in myself or someone else yesterday, I take heart, for today is a new beginning for us all.

And the beauty of living in the now is discovering so much more of God in me and God in my world.

> "See, now is the acceptable time; see,
> now is the day of salvation!"
> —2 Corinthians 6:2

Day 272

—◆—

God's loving grace is the foundation on which I build my life.

FOUNDATION OF GRACE — I may have wondered about people who, from all appearances, have built their lives around one person or one purpose, only to be hurt or disappointed when that person was gone or circumstances changed.

Loving relationships and achievements enrich my life, but I do not let them become my sole reason for existence. It is in God—enfolded in divine grace—that I will find true happiness and peace.

People change, circumstances change, *I* change, but God never changes. By the grace of God, I have all that I could ever desire—and more. And God's love is such that I will never be denied true joy. So I am grateful that God's grace is the foundation of my life, and I am grateful that I can look forward to lasting peace.

"According to the grace of God given to me, like a skilled master builder I laid a foundation."
—1 Corinthians 3:10

Day 273

—◆—

I live life as a celebration of the
divine life within me!

CELEBRATION
Right now, somewhere in the world, someone is celebrating a birthday and giving thanks for the miracle of life.

Life truly is a miracle—God's miraculous gift to all. The life that is within every tissue and cell of my body is filled with the energy of Spirit. I am richly nourished with the love, the beauty, and the wonder that God is in me.

So why only celebrate a birthday one day out of the year? Why not celebrate life every day? *I can!* I can make every day a day for giving thanks—for the life of God within me and for the healing it makes possible.

Divine life is so powerful that it can heal any condition! And certainly the life of God within me is worth celebrating—birthday or not. So I celebrate!

"They shall celebrate the fame of your abundant goodness, and shall sing aloud of your righteousness."
—Psalm 145:7

Day 274

—◆—

*I am refreshed and renewed by the
indwelling spirit of God.*

REFRESHED   I may enjoy being with people, especially the people I love; however, time alone can be a refreshing break.

In a few moments of quiet, I turn within to the divine spirit of my being and feel enfolded in peace, love, and understanding. As I allow my body to relax and my mind to become still, I feel a surge of spiritual energy from within.

In the sacred meeting place of my soul, I am in the presence of pure life and love. Any tense muscles relax, and my body is nourished by the peace I feel.

And even when I come back and continue with whatever it is I am doing, the peace from my sacred meeting place permeates the very air around me. I am refreshed and renewed.

**"Now when Jesus heard this, he withdrew from there in a
boat to a deserted place by himself."
—Matthew 14:13**

Day 275

—◆—

*Thank You, God, for the new me that is
emerging—every day!*

NEW ME

I have the power to change the
things about me that I truly desire to
change. So in a quiet time away from
the busyness of the day, I relax. I
concentrate on me—not in a self-centered way, but in
a Spirit-centered dedication of giving my time and
attention to the presence of God within me.

I concentrate on doing a great work on myself, not
on trying to change the people around me. I know that
it is up to each individual to work with God to change
the things he or she wants to change.

So I focus on changing me. Instead of reacting with
emotion to things that happen, I respond from the
spiritual center within me. Thank God that a new me is
emerging—a stronger, more faith-filled person.

"There is a new creation: everything old has passed
away; see, everything has become new!
All this is from God, who . . . has given us the
ministry of reconciliation."
—2 Corinthians 5:17–18

Day 276

—◆—

God has created me to be creative!

CREATIVE IMAGINING For a moment I imagine that I am a time traveler and I am there, centuries ago, by Michelangelo's side as he begins to turn a block of stone into a statue. It is amazing how this great artist keeps on chipping away—never giving up until a magnificent statue of David or Moses finally emerges.

Well, perhaps today I am working on my own block of stone—an idea or a dream that is slowly taking shape. And like Michelangelo, I will not give up on creating something magnificent, for God has given *me* the ability to create as well.

I may or may not produce a work of art. My special ability may be in creating a cheerful atmosphere wherever I am or in discovering a way to feed the world so that no one goes hungry. Or just maybe my warm embrace will turn someone's tears into a smile.

"When you send forth your spirit, they are created."
—Psalm 104:30

Day 277

—◆—

I touch the life of God,
and I soar to new heights!

ENDLESS POSSIBILITIES
There is great strength and intelligence within me that is generated by God, the one power in the universe. Intelligence and strength are in every atom of my body as ever-renewing life. The spirit of God dwells within me, waiting for me to tap into an unlimited supply of strength and wisdom.

In my prayer time, I turn within and listen as God directs me. With faith and assurance that God is pure wisdom, I draw upon divine power. The strength I need is readily absorbed into every fiber of my body, and I look to the endless possibilities that lie before me.

Through prayer—a time of speaking and listening, a sacred time of giving praise and receiving guidance—I touch the life of God within me and soar to new heights of strength and understanding.

> **"Be renewed in the spirit of your minds, and . . .**
> **clothe yourselves with the new self."**
> **—Ephesians 4:23–24**

Day 278

—◆—

I am a spiritual being living out my true reality.

TRUE REALITY

When I truly know who I am, I can live the truth of my reality. That truth is this: I am a spiritual being.

So instead of thinking or speaking of myself in terms of weakness or limitation, I think and speak of strength, for I draw upon the reservoir of spiritual strength that is within me. How can I be sure that it is always there? I can because I have been created with that spark of divinity within me.

When I have decisions to make or tests to complete, I have the wisdom and understanding to do my best. And prayer is part of my preparation for any project, test, or situation. In times of prayer, I gain new insight into the real me—the spiritual being who is capable, loving, peaceful, and ready for whatever is happening next.

"You have stripped off the old self with its practices and have clothed yourselves with the new self."
—Colossians 3:9–10

Day 279

—◆—

I listen to the indwelling spirit of God, a voice of wisdom and courage.

GOD, I AM LISTENING

I expect the unexpected, knowing that every single day will not go by without some surprises. But instead of listening to dire predictions or doubts, I speak to God and listen to the voice of my indwelling spirit:

"God, You are the voice of wisdom and courage. As I surrender to You, Your spirit within soothes my heart and clears away any confusion in my thoughts.

"I know that You will never forsake me, that You will always love me. So it is in this environment of trust, acceptance, and love that I become still and listen.

"What I hear may not be an audible voice, but a sure knowing that transcends the ability of my senses. God, here I am, and I am listening. . . . "

"The sound of the wings of the cherubim was heard as far as the outer court, like the voice of God Almighty when he speaks."
—Ezekiel 10:5

Day 280

—◆—

My loving words and kind actions make a heart connection with others.

LANGUAGE OF THE HEART "In everything do to others as you would have them do to you." This is the Golden Rule, and when I use it as the standard for all my actions, I cannot help but make a heart connection with the people whom I work, live, and interact with on a daily basis. Such a connection transcends disagreements, overcomes all obstacles, and promotes a universal language of love.

When my mind is filled with thoughts of God, my heart is filled with love. Then my words are naturally loving and kind. God *is* love. So as I speak loving words, I am inviting the spirit of God to speak through me to bless others.

When I follow the Golden Rule, I am following in the footsteps of the Master Teacher and speaking a language of the heart, a language of love.

"Out of the abundance of the heart the mouth speaks."
—Matthew 12:34

Day 281

—◆—

*I bring an awareness of God's order into this
day, and I am blessed.*

**AWARENESS
OF GOD**
There may be times when my life
seems to be anything but in a state of
divine order. Yet I know from experience that such times are temporary,
that God's perfect order is always present and active in
my life.

Any time that I feel out of sorts, that things are not
going as I would like them to go, I remember this verse
from Corinthians: "God is a God not of disorder but
of peace."

And this affirmation of truth blesses me every time I
think it or say it. By affirming the truth, I am taking my
focus off the challenge and bringing an awareness of
God into whatever I am doing.

Soon I will begin to see the order that is all around
me. I know that God is working with me, so I focus
my thoughts on divine order. Because I am focused, I
literally feel the presence of God's order and peace.

**"God is a God not of disorder but of peace."
—1 Corinthians 14:33**

Day 282

---◆---

The care I give others is from the love of God within me.

LIFE OF CARING

If I were to view my life as an unfolding story, what would I consider my most important accomplishments?

Would they be the things I have worked really hard for, or would they be the times I have put aside some important work to do something even more important, such as spending time with a child or an adult who needs someone to listen and to care?

The way I treat people may be the most important and inspiring part of my life story. Because I care for others, I love with a love that unites me with them. Because I care, I take extra notice of friends and strangers alike and appreciate that they are living examples of God's creative power and glory. Yes, I care, and because I do, a whole world of wonder opens to me.

> **"Let the little children come to me, and do not stop them; for it is to such as these that the kingdom of heaven belongs."**
> **—Matthew 19:14**

Day 283

—◆—

My prayers are united and in concert
with the prayers of others.

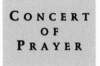

CONCERT OF PRAYER

The notes emanating from an orchestra as players tune their instruments are not in harmony. Although played at the same time, the notes are not in sync. However, once the conductor's baton begins the tempo, the resulting melody is a harmonious blending of notes in concert.

The same is true for me when I am in accord with the will and the work of God. My individual prayer support is, indeed, powerful, but when united with the thoughts and prayers of others around the world, the once single current of energy becomes a mighty power.

I unite with others in a concert of prayer. Our prayers bless us and reach out from us to bless the world.

"So shall my word be that goes out from my mouth;
it shall not return to me empty."
—Isaiah 55:11

Day 284

—◆—

*The spirit of God within is my
guiding light.*

**GUIDING
LIGHT**

The light at the end of the tunnel is a
radiant light that signals that the end of
darkness is near. So if events in my
own life leave me feeling as if I am in
the dark, I know to look toward the light. I know that
there will always be a light shining for me—the light of
the indwelling spirit of God.

The presence of God within shines forth as a light
of wisdom that can never be extinguished. My divine
connection with God and with God's love for me can
never be interrupted. An inner knowing assures me
that God is always with me, leading me into the light
of a new day.

When I trust God and rely on the inner presence of
God for inspiration and guidance, I know that the darkness of doubt and confusion cannot last long. In the
light of God, I know I will always find my way.

**"God is light and in him there is no darkness at all."
—1 John 1:5**

Day 285

—◆—

I am whole and holy, for I am strong in mind, body, and spirit.

WHOLE AND HOLY

I have had those mountaintop experiences. Maybe I was not at the top of an actual mountain, but I reached the heightened awareness that I am whole and holy. The exhilaration I felt was a rejoicing of my whole self—mind, body, and spirit.

And that kind of whole-self realization is what brings me to the mountaintop today. I experience what it is to call on spiritual power, the spirit of God within me, and to feel that response flooding my soul.

I think, pray, and act, knowing that the spirit of God renews my strength, guides my way, and empowers me. I am whole, and that wholeness includes wisdom and understanding, physical strength and endurance. All this I receive from the indwelling spirit of God.

"Be transformed by the renewing of your minds,
so that you may discern what is the will of God—
what is good and acceptable and perfect."
—Romans 12:2

Day 286

◆

God is my partner, so every work I do is a labor of love.

LABOR OF LOVE

I am amazed at how quickly time goes by when I am doing something I really enjoy. It does not matter where I am—at home or at work, in a class or in a meeting—because when I love what I am doing, I am naturally more creative and more willing to put my best efforts into doing it and doing it well. It is a true labor of love.

I realize that whatever I do can be a labor of love when I include God. God is my spiritual partner, and I am an instrument through which God brings some great blessings into the world.

So whatever my particular skills or specialties may be, I see them as gifts from God, gifts that are needed and important. Everything I do affects my world, so I take an active interest in my partnership with God and make whatever I do a labor of love!

"The Father who dwells in me does his works."
—John 14:10

Day 287

—◆—

With God as my teacher,
I am constantly learning.

LEARNING As a child, I was sent to school to learn, and I did learn some important facts and skills that helped me live as an adult in a complex world. But along my way in life, I discovered that learning does not end as soon as I receive a diploma, begin a career, or take on adult responsibilities.

In God's glorious world, every day is an opportunity to learn more about myself and others. I am constantly learning and growing, and my greatest growth comes with my own spiritual awareness.

I am a student of life, eager and open to learning from God, my supreme teacher. And if I should make what seems like an error, I recognize it as a growth experience. With God as my teacher, I am constantly learning and growing.

> **"Lead me in your truth, and teach me,**
> **for you are the God of my salvation."**
> **—Psalm 25:5**

Day 288

—◆—

The spirit of God lives in me. I am strong in the strength of spirit.

STRENGTH OF SPIRIT Oh, what a feeling of power surges through me when I know that, by the spirit of God dwelling in me, I am mightier than any challenge or circumstance! I rise to the occasion—whatever it may be—because the spirit of God lives in me!

If at some future time I believe that I have to be stronger in order to meet some challenge or go through a time of change, I remind myself that God in me is strength of spirit. Such divine strength is constantly energizing and renewing me.

And the wonder of it all is that I grow stronger as I let my awareness of God in me increase. Through the spirit of God, I am strong. I can do what I am inspired to do because God is my inspiration and all that I need to accomplish anything. *Yes,* I am strong in the strength of Spirit!

> "Not by might, nor by power, but by my spirit,
> says the Lord of hosts."
> —Zechariah 4:6

Day 289

—◆—

God, I realize the wonder of Your spirit
emerging from me.

TEACH ME

God, I pray that, in all that I do, Your will is being fulfilled. I know that You are in charge, that Your perfect order is at work to bring about peace. So I let go and let a divine work be done through me.

God, show me how to be a blessing to others. I am letting go now so that You can teach me to do Your will. I am letting go of what *appears* to be true and holding on to what I *know* is true—the rightness of Your will and Your way. As I do, I begin to see evidence of Your presence all around me—no matter how fast-paced and complicated the world may seem.

Thank You, God, for Your unfailing wisdom, love, and peace. As I let go, I realize the wonder of Your spirit as it emerges from me and in my world!

> **"Teach me to do your will,**
> **for you are my God."**
> **—Psalm 143:10**

Day 290

—◆—

*I lovingly share planet earth with all
God's creatures.*

**ALL GOD'S
CREATURES**
I can only begin to imagine what life would be like without the blessing of animal friends. Animals provide people with so much—companionship, unconditional love, and even music, for the song of a bird is music to my ears.

I think of pet owners who love and cherish pets as their faithful friends, park rangers who maintain safe environments for wild animals, and members of a family who visit the zoo. No matter who we are, we all have opportunities to interact with God's creatures in some way.

So I do all that I can to act responsibly toward every animal with which I share planet earth.

I bless all of God's creatures in my prayers, knowing that they, too, are creations of God.

**"In wisdom you have made them all;
the earth is full of your creatures."
—Psalm 104:24**

Day 291

$\longrightarrow \blacklozenge \longrightarrow$

I am an expression of God's love.

EXPRESSION OF LOVE   If I am sitting near someone, I might turn and look at that person, or if I am alone, I might hold a picture of a friend or loved one in mind. The person I am looking at or thinking of does not look exactly like me, but I use spiritual vision to look beyond appearances. Then I will see a person who is exactly like me—an expression of God's love to the world.

This I know is true: We are all expressions of God's love. No matter what color our skin is, what region of the world we live in, what our life choices are—we are all one and the same. We are all children of God.

God loves each of us equally, and as I look past any preconceived notions I may have about others, I will see that they were created by the same divine love that created me.

> **"Jesus said . . . 'Peace be with you.**
> **As the Father has sent me, so I send you.' "**
> **—John 20:21**

Day 292

—◆—

The creative life of God is restoring me, healing me, and nurturing me.

CREATIVE LIFE

I dedicate my thoughts and my prayers to an awareness of the health and wholeness of God-life within me. I know that no matter what conditions or symptoms may be, the life of God within me is oh, so much greater. So I call on the greater life that is within me now.

The very life of God—the energy and intelligence of the Creator—is at the core of every cell of my heart, my legs, my arms, my whole body. Creative life in all its glory is healing and nurturing me.

I know that anything that attempts to alter the expression of life by me and through me is now dissolved. With every fiber of my being, I know that I was created to be an expression of the God-life within me. Answering this higher calling, I celebrate the life of God that is within me and that is expressing through me.

"Your wounds I will heal."
—Jeremiah 30:17

Day 293

—◆—

God is the source of the love, understanding, and caring between friends.

FRIEND

Friends are special people with whom I share my hopes, my dreams, and my life. My friends may be family, co-workers, classmates, and neighbors, but whoever they are, we are united in a circle of love and prayer that keeps us close and in touch no matter how much distance separates us.

So whenever I am away from my friends or they are away from me, I remind myself that God's presence is at the core of each of us. The Holy Presence unites us— one friend with another.

Whenever and wherever loving, caring people come together, God is the "friend" in their friendships. God is the source of love, understanding, and caring that transpires between friends. What I love, revere, and connect with in my friends is truly divine.

"I have called you friends, because I have made known to you everything that I have heard from my Father."
—John 15:15

Day 294

—◆—

*In silence with God, I rediscover
my divine potential.*

At times I may feel as if something is
lacking in my life, that there is more
which I should be experiencing. But by
entering into the silence with God, the
questions of my heart will be answered, and I will once
again reconnect with divine wisdom.

In silence, I remember that I am a spiritual being
living a human experience. As I tap into my spiritual
center and rediscover the truth of my being, I recognize
that I am whole in spirit, mind, and body.

In silence, my spiritual nature is revealed to me, and I
rediscover my divine potential: I am created in the
image and likeness of God. I continue on my human
journey aware of who I am and why I am here, knowing that God-life within me is my reality.

In silence with God, I rediscover my divine potential.

"God created humankind in his image. . . .
and indeed, it was very good."
—Genesis 1:27, 31

Day 295

—◆—

Through the spirit of God within me,
I am capable of achieving my goals.

CAPABLE

Do I believe that I can achieve whatever I set out to accomplish? *I can!* Through the spirit of God within me, I am capable of achieving all my goals—and so very much more!

The indwelling spirit of God is a spark of divinity within me. When I turn to God, I am connected with a spiritual battery that charges me up and gives me all the energy and motivation I could ever need to set my goals and then to act on them.

So I make turning to God for guidance and inspiration my dedication. By doing so, I am laying the groundwork for success in any project I undertake.

When the basics are there, everything else will naturally fall into place. And touching base with the spirit of God within me is the most basic of all my needs.

> "Jesus said to him, 'If you are able!—
> All things can be done for the one who believes.' "
> —Mark 9:23

Day 296

◆

I give my loved ones the gift of my faith-filled prayers today.

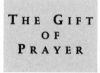

THE GIFT OF PRAYER

I dedicate this message to my loved ones: "I said a prayer for you today. You may not have known that I was thinking of you at that moment, but perhaps you felt the reassurance of God's love and my own.

"I said a prayer for you today, for your well-being, your peace of mind, your strength of spirit. The greatest gift I can give to you is my prayers, and I gladly do so, knowing that God's presence is active in your life.

"I said a prayer to God today and gave thanks to the One who created such a masterpiece. You are God's child, and I could not ask for a greater Protector for you than God.

"I said a prayer for myself today, a prayer that I may always know your friendship and love in my life.

"I said a prayer for you today, because I love you and I care."

**"I am asking on their behalf . . .
because they are yours."
—John 17:9**

Day 297

—◆—

New birth replenishes the world, and rebirth nourishes my soul.

BIRTH AND REBIRTH

Right at this moment, children are being born, and fresh, new life is coming into the world. So I say: "God bless you, children, and welcome. Welcome to a world I cherish, live in, and share with you and with the whole family of God."

And there is rebirth going on also, for I am continually discovering or rediscovering my true identity. As magnificently as the physical body is designed, I am even greater than what I appear to be. At the core of the human form, I am a spiritual being, created in the image of God. I am a child of the Creator.

The rebirth I go through is a fantastic discovery of my own spirituality. I say to all others, "Welcome, child of God, to an awareness of who you are—a divine being on a spiritual quest."

**"What is born of the flesh is flesh,
and what is born of the Spirit is spirit."
—John 3:6**

Day 298

—◆—

In the quietness of my soul,
I listen to God's guidance.

I LISTEN

I have many choices to make each day, most of which I make without undue thought or consideration. But whether my decisions seem to be of little or of tremendous importance, I don't have to make them alone. I have the assurance of knowing that as I am willing to let it happen, God is my guide.

In the quietness of my soul, I listen to divine guidance and act with strength of mind in all my decisions. The far-reaching effects of God's loving counsel may not always be apparent in the decisions I make when I make them, but my time in prayer keeps me in tune with divine guidance and filters out any confusion.

I keep going, for God is there to take me by the hand and lead me onward.

"You hold my right hand.
You guide me with your counsel."
—Psalm 73:23–24

Day 299

---◆---

Thank You, God. I believe that with You all things are possible!

I BELIEVE!

God, I stood before you feeling lost and confused; You showed me the way. I desired forgiveness for something I had done; You gave me such assurance of Your love that I once more felt gloriously alive. I asked You to stay with me always; You assured me that You would never leave. You asked only that I have faith; I told You I believed.

God, You have given me so much, and the greatest gifts I can give to You are my faith and love, which I do wholeheartedly. You are my life, my everything—my every moment of the day, my every breath.

God, I believe that all things are possible through Your power, and I know that You are active in my life. I believe that You are with me now and always, and I am grateful. Thank You, God. I believe!

**"Before they call I will answer,
while they are yet speaking I will hear."
—Isaiah 65:24**

Day 300

---◆---

I have so much to give as I let the spirit of God give through me.

A SPIRIT OF GIVING

Rather than think about what I can take away from this day, I think about what God has given me to bring to this day.

I bring a loving heart to this day. Whatever it is that I do, whomever I interact with, I know that as I let love be a part of it all, there are tremendous blessings in store.

I bring a willingness to listen to others to this day. I truly hear the child, spouse, friend, or teacher whom I may only have given my partial attention to yesterday. I understand there is so much to gain when one child of God is willing to listen to another child of God.

I bring a commitment to serve God to this day, and because I do, I also bring a sacred blessing to every relationship, situation, or circumstance. It is true—I have much to give as I let the spirit of God give through me!

"Give, and it will be given to you."
—Luke 6:38

Day 301

God goes with me into new places, activities, and responsibilities.

GOD GOES WITH ME My loved ones or I myself may be leaving home, traveling to new cities, schools, or jobs. I understand that this time of moving on does not have to lessen that strong connection of love and faith that we share with each other.

If I am moving on, one of the most comforting and loving things I can do for myself is to know and affirm: *God goes with me into new places, new activities, and new responsibilities.*

If loved ones are moving or traveling, I know and affirm for them: *God goes with you into new places, new activities, and new responsibilities.* As I release them, I envision them blessed and at peace, guided by God wherever they go and in whatever they do.

> **"But for me it is good to be near God;
> I have made the Lord God my refuge."
> —Psalm 73:28**

Day 302

◆

In prayer, I tune in to the will of God.

 A TIME OF PRAYER
Just as I customize my own wardrobe with items that fit me and my style, I also choose the way I pray so that it meets my individual needs.

My times of prayer are as unique and individual as I am. I may pray out loud and with great enthusiasm, or, at other times, I might prefer turning within for a time of quiet meditation and reflection.

No one can tell me exactly the right way to pray. So I rely on the spirit of God within me to guide me to the way that is right for me.

As I pray, I relinquish my concerns to God and know that a power far greater than me is in charge. If I were to tell God what I wanted the answer to be, I would be limiting myself, for there may be more options available than I could ever begin to conceive as possible. So I pray, "God, Your will be done."

"Your will be done."
—Matthew 6:10

Day 303

—◆—

*Immersed in the presence of God, I am filled
with the peace of God.*

**SACRED
PRESENCE**
Dear God, I come to You in prayer
to be refreshed. Immersed in Your
presence, I am connected with the
inner peace that You have created me
to know and express.

In the sacred silence with You, I find relief from the
sounds and sights and pressures of my day. And I realize that as I become still, as I relax, I open myself to a
flow of peace that is there waiting to ease any anxiety,
to quiet any fear.

Right now in this moment, I let inner peace—divine
tranquillity—rise up to meet me and to relieve all concern. From the depths of my soul, I feel a surge of serenity moving through me, relaxing my muscles, calming
my thoughts.

Immersed in Your presence, God, I understand that
this is where I can always come and be filled with
peace divine.

**"Peace I leave with you; my peace I give to you."
—John 14:27**

Day 304

—◆—

Praise God, I am loved with everlasting, unconditional love.

GOD LOVES ME

God's love is a love that I can be absolutely sure of at all times. It is true: God loves me! God is love, and God lives within me as love everlasting.

Right now, I allow myself to feel the love of God stirring within me. I say softly and tenderly, "God loves me." I say it again, and then, for a moment, I rest in the presence of pure love and let it wash over me. I know how wonderful it feels to be loved with unconditional love!

There is nothing in the past, present, or future that can keep God's love from me. I know this is true as I open my heart and soul to the spirit of God as pure love. In the warm glow of God's love, I find healing, understanding, direction, and all the richness of Spirit that I could ever desire.

> **"I trust in the steadfast love of God**
> **forever and ever."**
> **—Psalm 52:8**

Day 305

—◆—

Prayer nourishes my soul.

NOURISH THE SOUL I know how important it is to feed my body nourishing foods and to get plenty of exercise and rest. Such actions help my body to be as healthy as it was created to be and to perform in peak condition.

It is equally important to feed my soul with the kind of nourishment it needs so that I can maintain a healthy balance in my spirit, soul, and body. I feed my soul with divine ideas that stimulate creative actions by spending time in prayer with God.

In prayer, I give thanks for the marvelous abilities of my body and for the smooth and efficient way it functions. And I am equally grateful for the nourishment for my soul that I receive in this sacred time with God. Blessed by God, I express my appreciation: "Thank You, God, for nourishing my soul!"

> "Beloved, I pray that all may go well with
> you and that you may be in good health, just
> as it is well with your soul."
> —3 John 1:2

Day 306

—◆—

*I behold the glory and wonder of God's splendor
all around me!*

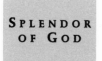

**SPLENDOR
OF GOD**

Towering trees, flowering meadows, dancing seas—all are examples of God's glory and splendor. How beautiful and awe-inspiring is the world in which I live!

Now I look a little closer to home to catch a glimpse of the splendor and wonder of God that is written on the face of every person I meet. God's brilliance shines forth from friends and strangers alike, reminding me to let my own light shine. When I do, I am truly a beacon of God's love and goodwill.

From the beauty of nature to the diversity of every human face, everything is an expression of God's splendor. I can feel the excitement building as I anticipate the other wonders that are even now unfolding in my life!

**"They shall speak of the glory of your kingdom . . .
to make known to all people your mighty deeds,
and the glorious splendor of your kingdom."
—Psalm 145:11–12**

Day 307

◆

God, You are my all, and I have absolute faith in You.

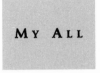

MY ALL

God, I know that Your will is constantly being carried out, and because of this, I need never fear what lies ahead for me. My future is secure because, in every moment, You are with me, guiding me as I live out a divine plan.

The world around me may change, but Your presence remains a constant in my life. Heart and soul, I have faith enough to follow where You lead me.

You do not judge me, nor will You ever forsake me. For this and so many other blessings, I am grateful. In Your eyes there is no wrong which cannot be righted, no offense which cannot be rectified.

I live my life totally believing in You and dedicating my every word, action, and deed to Your greatness. You are more than I need and all that I desire. God, You are my all, and I am grateful.

"We walk by faith, not by sight."
—2 Corinthians 5:7

DAILY WORD

Day 308

◆

*God's joy fills me and overflows from
me to others.*

**GOD IS
JOY**

I begin to smile when I think about
what happens when people start to
laugh. Their eyes light up, they smile,
and their entire body responds as they
give in to the joy of the moment.

Science has proven the health benefits of laughter,
but there are other benefits as well. I know that laughter
puts me in touch with the spirit of God within. God *is*
joy, so expressing joy is letting God move through me
to bring happiness to others.

God's joy fills me and overflows from me to others!
It is natural to want to share my joy with others, to
share love, laughter, and goodwill. I am in tune with the
spirit of God within me, and my joy helps create a rip-
ple effect that spreads out in joy and gladness to others.

**"Our mouth was filled with laughter,
and our tongue with shouts of joy."
—Psalm 126:2**

Day 309

—◆—

*At home with God, I find rest
and renewal.*

 I hear a gentle urging: "Wherever you are right now, whatever you are doing, come away for a while and rest. Come away by tuning out any noise and confusion that are going on around you, and retreat to the inner sanctuary of your soul."

This retreat is a homecoming for me. There is nothing, absolutely nothing, I need to do except allow myself to be with God. I feel, more than hear, the gentle whisper of Spirit saying, "Here, My beloved, I give you rest."

As if by some mystery, all that ever concerned me before is now gone. Any physical discomfort has ceased, and I feel a rush of new energy.

I return to my day knowing that I can come home to be with God as quickly and easily as I make the decision to do so. With God, I rest and I am refreshed.

"Come away to a deserted place all by yourselves and rest a while."
—Mark 6:31

Day 310

—◆—

I appreciate and enjoy being a student in the great school of life.

STUDENT OF LIFE

Even though I may not be officially enrolled in school, I am a student—a student of life and truth.

Life is an education in itself, and I may feel at times as if I am being tested. When this happens, I hold to the truth I know: God is with me, and through God's loving spirit within, I can overcome any challenge.

Every challenge is a learning experience that moves me another step forward in my growing awareness of God's presence in my life. So while I give each person or situation consideration, I know that God is in charge.

An important part of learning is being able to enjoy and appreciate the process. And I will enjoy everything that much more when I realize that I am a student in the great school of life!

> "Teach me the way I should go,
> for to you I lift up my soul."
> —Psalm 143:8

Day 311

—◆—

I am a sacred being, for God's spirit expresses itself through me.

SACRED BEING

Something powerful is stirring within me, and it is more than a thought or a feeling. It is a belief in sacredness as the foundation of my own mind and body. It is knowing that the spirit of God within me infuses me with life and energy.

I am a sacred, spiritual being clothed in a body of life and created with a mind of unlimited understanding. So no matter what is happening *to* me, what is most meaningful for me to remember is what is happening *within* me.

God's spirit refreshes and sustains me. I have wholeness of body, peace of mind, and power of Spirit with me at all times. Yes, that sacred stirring builds into a sureness of God in me and God expressing through me.

"To them God chose to make known how great among the Gentiles are the riches of the glory of this mystery, which is Christ in you, the hope of glory."
—Colossians 1:27

Day 312

---◆---

In every season, I am alive with the life of God.

SEASONS

If I were to come upon an apple tree in the middle of winter, I might think from the looks of its bare branches that this tree will never again bloom and bear fruit. Yet when I return to that same tree in the spring, the beauty and fragrance of its blossoms will fairly shout: "I am alive!"

Just as the appearance of the apple tree changes with the seasons, so does my appearance change. Yet such appearances do not tell the truth about me. If I am going through a season that seems bare because of a challenge, I have hope because I know that God's spirit within me is alive.

And because God's spirit is within me, life, joy, and wisdom are ready to burst forth and declare, *"Yes, I am alive with the life of God!"*

> **"The spirit of God has made me,**
> **and the breath of the Almighty gives me life."**
> **—Job 33:4**

Day 313

—◆—

Thank You, God, for everything.

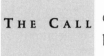

THE CALL God, Your presence in my life is dearer to me than I could ever hope to put into mere words.

I am blessed in knowing that You are aware of my love for You, that You hear every whisper of love from my heart.

When I call for You, I know You will answer, for You are my loving parent—a parent who always cares for and nurtures me. I know with a knowledge born of faith that You will never leave me.

I give my all to You. With every waking moment, I dedicate my life, my thoughts, and my actions to living my divine potential.

I give thanks to You now for guiding me when I seemed lost, for loving me when I thought I was unlovable, and for filling me with peace when I felt there was none to be found. Thank You, God!

"I will counsel you with my eye upon you."
—Psalm 32:8

Day 314

—◆—

*God, You are the answer to my
every prayer.*

**GOD IS
THE
ANSWER**
God, You have heard my call, and I
feel the reassurance of Your answer. In
the silence of my soul, I listen to the
still, small voice that speaks volumes to
me and leads me to a realm of endless possibilities in a
world of great potential.

God, Your reassurance lifts my heart and mind above
any challenge and gently, tenderly releases me into a
realm of peace and security.

Whatever my prayer—healing, prosperity, serenity—I
rest in the assurance that You will always answer.
Through Your comforting presence, my faith grows and
all concerns fade in the light of that faith.

God, I called and You answered, for You *are* the
answer—to my every question, to my every prayer.

**"Call to me and I will answer you, and will tell you
great and hidden things that you have not known."
—Jeremiah 33:3**

Day 315

—◆—

I value the presence of God in me and in all creation.

SOMETHING OF VALUE
Do I look for the value instead of the flaws in people and situations? Maybe I have not always been a value seeker, but from this moment on, I can and will be.

The very attitude of beholding the best in me, in others, and in circumstances is in itself a silent but powerful message that calls out strength, beauty, and truth.

And there is something of great value always ready to be expressed. God's spirit is present in every person, waiting to flow out as love and kindness, as comfort and support. God is present in the very atmosphere in which we live and move as a vital connection from one heart to another.

Because I value the spirit of God, I value everyone and everything in God's creation.

"The kingdom of heaven is like a merchant in search of fine pearls; on finding one pearl of great value, he went and sold all that he had and bought it."
—Matthew 13:45–46

Day 316

—◆—

My soul sings a song of joy in God.

JOY OF MY SOUL Joy is a celebration of the soul that resounds throughout my body in a song of gladness. This song of joy is beyond words and sounds; it is the very life of God vibrating within me.

Such joy of the soul stirs up healing of my body and emotions. I may never realize just how tense I have been until the joy of God courses through me and sweeps away any resistance to life and gladness.

I am always singing on key and in tune when I sing a song from my soul. It is a wake-up call to blessing after blessing—a silent yet powerful song of prayer that awakens me to the joy that God has already given me to experience and express.

> "O God, you are my God, I seek you. . . .
> For you have been my help, and in the
> shadow of your wings I sing for joy."
> —Psalm 63:1, 7

Day 317

—◆—

*Divine wisdom and love are the golden threads
that weave us all together.*

**G O L D E N
T H R E A D**

I have gone to school to learn, yet there are many things I know intuitively without being taught. I know because I am one with God, one with the wisdom of the universe.

Divine wisdom and love are golden threads that weave me together with others. We are all one with God. As God's creations, we are divinely connected—one with divine love and wisdom, one with each other. We share a unity of purpose that forges a bond between us and calls us ever higher, ever forward on our journey through life.

So today and every day, I let God love through me. As I do, I am strengthening my bond with my worldwide family and laying a firm foundation that can never be destroyed.

"You desire truth in the inward being;
therefore teach me wisdom in my secret heart."
—Psalm 51:6

Day 318

—◆—

My faith increases in an ever-growing awareness of God.

FAITH

God, how could I not have faith in You, the Creator of a glorious universe filled with wonder and delight.

And, God, I am so thankful for Your love and care. I am amazed at the extent of Your care when warm rays of sunshine that have traveled through the vastness of space touch my face. When a child reaches out in the joy of loving and touches me, I feel a greater understanding of my faith in You and Your unconditional love for me.

Yes, my faith in You increases with my growing awareness of Your presence. As I discover more and more of the wonder and delight of Your creation, I understand that You are saying, "I am with you and within you always." God, I am thankful for You and thankful for my ever-growing awareness of Your presence.

"Jesus answered them, 'Have faith in God.' "
—Mark 11:22

Day 319

—◆—

*I thank God for being my faithful,
loving companion.*

**BLESSED
JOURNEY**
I am on my own special path in life, and my journey, not my arrival, is what is important. Every day of my journey, I give and receive blessings.

Even in the most challenging of times, when it seems I am required to go the extra mile, I find that I can do it. I discover that I have more courage, wisdom, and strength than I ever before dreamed I had.

I have more because God is replacing whatever I use even faster than I can use it. So I take time to savor every day of my journey.

I have taken my path not by chance, but because I have divine appointments to keep. And I know that God is my companion all along the way.

"As he was setting out on a journey, a man ran up and
knelt before him, and asked him, 'Good Teacher, what
must I do to inherit eternal life?' "
—Mark 10:17

Day 320

—◆—

*I am an instrument of God's peace
and harmony in my world.*

SONG OF PEACE
A musical instrument cannot play itself, but in the hands of a master musician, it seems to come alive with beautiful, soul-stirring music.

We ourselves are instruments through which God produces beautiful music, songs of peace and harmony, for those around us to enjoy. As instruments of peace, we are continually sharing the blessings of God's love that lives in our own hearts and minds.

The love and peace of God are waiting to play through us in an uplifting harmony of tranquil thoughts, words, and actions. Being God's instruments of peace, we understand that we are eternally one with the serenity of God.

In harmony with the peace of God within us, within others, and all around us, we bring every person on earth into our song of peace.

"Create in me a clean heart, O God."
—Psalm 51:10

Day 321

—◆—

*God, the wonder of Your grace fills
me with awe.*

**WONDER
OF GOD'S
GRACE**

God, when I thought I had reached
my lowest point, You lifted me higher
than I ever imagined possible. Because
You love me, You caught me each time
I stumbled and started to fall.

I thought I had seen all the beauty there was to see,
but each day You show me more of the wonders Your
world has to offer. Your grace fills me with such awe
and wonder that I feel humbled.

When I thought I had been loved by another and
then been disappointed, You showed me what true love
really is. I did not need to ask for Your love, it was
already mine—given freely and unconditionally to me.

God, Your glory is everywhere, and I accept and
joyously give thanks for the wonder of Your grace.

**"Did I not tell you that if you believed,
you would see the glory of God?"
—John 11:40**

Day 322

—◆—

I breathe deeply of the breath of life and the freedom of Spirit.

FREEDOM OF SPIRIT   I take in one breath at a time, and each breath nourishes my body. The less concern I have about breathing, the easier each breath comes. I breathe deeply of the breath of life.

And so it is with my freedom. I take in the reality of my freedom one moment at a time. I do not struggle with freedom from any habit or condition when I relax and know that I am divinely empowered. I breathe deeply of the freedom of Spirit.

I let the awareness of my freedom in God fill my mind and my body. Now my focus is on freedom, and any tendency to want or need something more dissipates in the freshness of spiritual freedom.

I breathe deeply of the breath of life and the freedom of Spirit that God is constantly pouring out to me.

"As servants of God, live as free people."
—1 Peter 2:16

Day 323

—◆—

In the silence of prayer, I am aware of my oneness with God.

SILENCE OF PRAYER

In the silence of prayer, I enter a sacred meeting place where only joy and love and peace exist.

In silence, I meet with God, who welcomes me with open arms. Lovingly, tenderly, I am surrounded and enfolded in a healing, radiating light—divine light—that can never be extinguished.

In silence, I am one with the wisdom, the love, and the peace of God. God's spirit flows in and through me in wave after wave, comforting me and renewing me in mind, body, and spirit.

In silence, I am aware of my oneness with God and with all creation. I understand that no matter where I am or where I go, God is with me.

God lives within me. I am one with God, and God is one with me.

"For God alone my soul waits in silence."
—Psalm 62:5

Day 324

—◆—

*I claim and give thanks for my
blessings now!*

**CLAIM
THE
BLESSINGS**

How can I keep what is important
to me from slipping away? I can by
remembering the truth: I am a beloved
child of God, and it is God's good
pleasure to give me the kingdom.

What is mine in spirit can never be taken away. So I
let go any fears I may have about losing some *thing* and
focus instead on claiming the abundance that God has
for me now.

As I claim and give thanks for my blessings, I am
making spiritual progress and letting God be involved
every step of the way. Each small step I take leads me to
a greater understanding of the many ways that God can
bless me.

Right now, I claim the blessings that only God can
supply and only God can lead me in discovering.

**"I will send down the showers in their season;
they shall be showers of blessing."
—Ezekiel 34:26**

Day 325

——◆——

*I am secure and at peace, for God's presence is
always with me.*

**ALWAYS
GOD**
Wherever I go and whatever I do, I
know that God is with me, that God
loves me. Divine love goes with me
even to the farthest points of the world.

I allow myself to feel secure, for God's love for me is
unfailing and without end. There is nothing I could
ever do that would separate me from God's loving,
protecting presence.

So I let go worries, I let go fears, I let go anything that
creates a doubt in my mind. I trust in God with all my
heart, and I experience peace that is divine.

Just as God is always with me, God is also with my
loved ones. I trust them to God's care and keeping and
know that they are enfolded in an everlasting love that
knows no bounds.

God is always with me and my loved ones, keeping
us secure and giving us rest.

> **"Know that I am with you and will keep you
> wherever you go."**
> **—Genesis 28:15**

Day 326

—◆—

God is the miracle-working power in my life.

MIRACLES

Some people might define miracles as blessings so incredible that odds are they will not happen to them. But if I consider the seeming miracles that occur every day—new life, the sunrise and sunset—I would see that miracles are more than a rarity—they are a reality. What may seem to be miraculous to some can easily be explained as the unlimited power of God.

Life is a miracle, and because all people have been created by the same Master Creator, we are all living, breathing miracles—examples of the infinite possibilities that are available to us through God.

Divine miracles are all around me, and through the miracles I experience every day, God encourages me to believe that all things are possible.

" 'I am the Alpha and the Omega,' says the Lord God,
who is and who was and who is to come,
the Almighty."
—Revelation 1:8

DAILY WORD

Day 327

—◆—

*The gentle spirit of God fills me
with peace.*

**GENTLE
SPIRIT**

No matter what is going on around me, the spirit of God is peace within that soothes and comforts me. So if I am faced with a challenge of monumental proportions or merely undecided about something, I know that I can rely on the sacred spirit of God.

The spirit of God is my divine connection with the peace that passes all understanding. I claim this peace as I spend time in prayer each day.

In prayer, I open my heart to my Creator. In the presence of God, I realize that outer distractions have no power over me. So I am at peace with myself and with all that is going on around me. I know that the decisions I make will be based on sound, spiritual understanding. I relax and let the spirit of God show me the wonder of life!

> **"I have said this to you, so that in me
> you may have peace."**
> **—John 16:33**

Day 328

—◆—

*God is the source of all blessings, and I am
abundantly blessed!*

**ABUNDANTLY
BLESSED**

How often do I find myself looking forward to a paycheck as if it
were the very source of all my prosperity? Yes, my income is important,
and I give thanks for it. But my paycheck and my
place of employment are simply channels for my
blessings. The source is God.

God is the source of blessings that come through
many different channels. So whether I define prosperity
as more money, healthy relationships, or even peace of
mind, I give thanks to God as the originator of it all.
Then I am always open to the new and creative ways
that my blessings can come to me.

I know that God is the source of all blessings, and I
am abundantly blessed!

"And God is able to provide you with every
blessing in abundance, so that by always having enough
of everything, you may share abundantly
in every good work."
—2 Corinthians 9:8

Day 329

—◆—

*The very essence of God permeates
my soul.*

SOUL

My activities and emotions may seem to drain my physical strength, but the vitality of my soul never wanes. My soul is a sacred home for the spirit of God.

The essence of God permeates my soul, and I am one with pure love and absolute knowledge. My soul is in tune with God's limitless light and love, and each time I turn to this light and love through my prayers and meditations, I reach new heights of awareness and energy. I have soared higher than I ever thought possible, for I have touched God.

My soul cooperates with my body to maintain the sanctity of God that lives within me. I reflect this goodness of God with every thought I think and with every action I take. The soul is a meeting place where I am aware that God and I are one.

"In him we live and move and have our being."
—Acts 17:28

Day 330

—◆—

I am a beautiful part of God's beautiful world.

CREATION OF BEAUTY
I have heard that beauty is in the eye of the beholder, so today and every day I make a conscious effort to behold the beauty in all people. Every person of every nation is a child of God, here by divine appointment.

All people—my friends, relatives, even complete strangers—are works of the divine Creator. They are all tributes to God's grandeur and reflect the beauty that is God.

I am beautiful. When I look in the mirror, I see a unique, magnificent, God-centered being looking back.

The wonderful planet and people whom God has created are as spiritually refreshing to my soul as they are pleasing to my eyes. My heart leaps in faith and love as I revel in being a beautiful part of God's beautiful world.

> **"You are in the Spirit, since the Spirit of
> God dwells in you."
> —Romans 8:9**

Day 331

—◆—

God, Your life within me lives out through me as strength and vitality.

HEALED!

God, in prayer, I enter consciously into an awareness of Your presence. I lift my thoughts, my voice to You in prayer, and my body responds with new surges of healing activity.

I am continually being healed as Your spirit within renews my body. Thank You for enlivening me with life. Your spirit is at the core of my body as life in diverse and wondrous expression.

I make prayer a part of my daily living by taking time each day to pray. And prayer takes on many forms: a thought of Your presence within me, words that declare life and healing, or an attitude of expecting a blessing.

God, my prayer is that I remain aware of Your presence, Your life living out through me as strength and vitality.

"The tongue of the wise brings healing."
—Proverbs 12:18

Day 332

—◆—

*Through the presence of God in me, I connect
with the order of the universe.*

**O R D E R
O F   T H E
U N I V E R S E**   God has the power to bring order
to seeming chaos, and I connect
with divine order through the power
of God's presence in me. Even in
what appears to be the most impossible situation,
order is possible, for divine order is bringing about
the right solutions.

Through the presence of God in me, I tap into the
inexhaustible source of divine energy, the divine energy
that establishes and maintains the universe. By affirming
that divine order is governing all creatures great and
small and ruling the stars, the moon, and the sun, I am
acknowledging that God is indeed in charge.

God's order rules not only my life but the entire
universe. As I cooperate with divine order, I will see
every situation unfolding in harmonious, orderly ways.

"Then God said, 'Let there be light';
and there was light."
—Genesis 1:3

Day 333

—◆—

Believing in God, I make this moment and any moment a time of prayer.

PRAYER MOMENT My prayer times are not limited to just the moments that I have set aside to consciously be in the presence of God. Rather, *any* moment of my life can be a prayer that offers confirmation of what I think and feel and believe.

So I speak words of love and truth. I think thoughts that are in line with what I know in my heart is true. And what I know is true is this: God loves me and is always ready to bless me in miraculous ways and by wondrous means!

I place my wholehearted belief in God and God's blessings—not in outer circumstances. Believing in God, how could I ever doubt that everything will work out in a divine way and through a divine plan?

"Do not worry about anything, but in everything by prayer and supplication with thanksgiving let your requests be made known to God."
—Philippians 4:6

Day 334

—◆—

*My prayer, God, is not my will, but Your
will be done.*

**SURRENDER
TO GOD**
If my life is not going along the way
I would like it to, it could be that I am
trying to force an outcome that may
not be the best one for me.

So rather than despair because things are not going
right, I take a moment to stop and turn the situation
over to God. I surrender my own will and let God's will
be done.

Surrendering to God is not giving up. Rather, it is
letting divine order take over and recognizing that God's
will is being done. By surrendering my life to God, I am
placing my trust in the one Power in the universe,
knowing that I am surrendering my will to the greater
will of God.

By inviting God to be an active participant in my life,
I am letting God be God in me. Surrendering to God is
a divine plan in living a fulfilling life.

> **"Submit yourselves therefore to God. . . .
> And he will draw near to you."
> —James 4:7, 8**

Day 335

—◆—

*I offer my prayers, my care, and my love for the
children of the world.*

**FOR THE
CHILDREN**
I probably will never get a better
glimpse of the future than when I look
into the faces of children. The children
who are playing at my feet or in my
neighborhood today will grow up to be caretakers of
the world. And I know within my own heart that,
whatever these children choose as their life's work, they
can never be less than beloved children of God.

And what better can I do for my family, my neighborhood, my world than to care for and about children?
Whether I am a parent, grandparent, teacher, or other
caregiver, I pray for children in faith and with unconditional love. I give the kind of care that allows children to
unfold their God-given abilities as gently and beautifully as a rose unfolds its petals for all to behold.

"Let the little children come to me,
and do not stop them; for it is to such as these
that the kingdom of heaven belongs."
—Matthew 19:14

Day 336

—◆—

There is a new and glorious me
emerging each day.

NEW BEGINNINGS

Every day, every moment is a new beginning. What a blessed relief it is to know that I can begin again, that I do not have to repeat the same mistakes over and over again. I can do so much better.

My new beginning may be in a different job, relationship, home, or school. Or, miracle of miracles, my new beginning may be in my *current* job, relationship, home, or school!

And I am always prepared for a new beginning when I dedicate my heart and soul, my activities and time to being part of a divine plan that is unfolding.

There is a new, wiser, healthier, more peaceful person emerging in my life every day. And what glory I feel in knowing that this new person is the real me!

"You have been born anew, not of perishable but
of imperishable seed, through the living and
enduring word of God."
—1 Peter 1:23

Day 337

—◆—

You are always in my thoughts and prayers.

ENVISIONING YOU BLESSED

One of the most helpful things I can do for others is to pray for them. So I am dedicating this day to praying for friends and family and for every member of the worldwide community. As I pray, I envision each one being blessed by my message of love:

"I love you. I appreciate all that you are and everything you do to bring your own special light into the world. You are one of God's own, a unique and wonderful expression of life and love.

"You are always in my thoughts and prayers. As I pray for you, I see you expressing the spirit of God in all that you do, in all that you are. I see you whole and free, healed of any condition that might hinder your progress on this journey we call life.

"Thank you for being you, and thank you for the blessing you are in my life."

"Pray for one another, so that you may be healed."
—James 5:16

Day 338

—◆—

I am empowered with the energy and strength of Spirit.

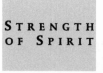

STRENGTH OF SPIRIT Divine power is mightier than any circumstance or situation, stronger than any person or thing. But how can I tap into this power and use it to grow stronger?

I do through the presence of God within me. In 1 Corinthians, Paul reminds all, "We proclaim Christ . . . the power of God and the wisdom of God." By turning to the indwelling spirit of God, I have access to divine power and to the wisdom I need to use it wisely.

The spirit of God goes with me wherever I go, so I always have the energy and strength I need to face any situation. I let go human doubts and let God fill my mind with the wisdom and understanding that will never fail me.

I am empowered with the energy and strength of God!

"You have given me wisdom and power."
—Daniel 2:23

Day 339

—◆—

I feel a oneness with all life and a reverence for all that God has created.

REVERENCE FOR LIFE I marvel at the beauty of a sunset as nature paints a brilliant masterpiece across the darkening sky. I cannot help but be inspired as I view nature in all its glory.

God's radiant glory is all around me. I see it in the natural order of the gently falling rain and in the spectacular beauty of a thunderstorm; I see God's love in the trusting smile of a young child. God is within everyone and everything, and because I realize this, I feel a oneness with all life and a reverence for all that God has created.

Every life on earth is an expression of God's creativity, and everything I see is a part of God. So I honor each person, each *life,* as one of God's awe-inspiring creations.

I shower others with love and respect. I truly see God's glory in my life and in the world.

**"Did I not tell you that if you believed,
you would see the glory of God?"
—John 11:40**

Day 340

—◆—

*In all that I do, I seek God and
God's blessings.*

SEEK GOD
No matter how full my life may
seem, I may feel that something important is missing. So when I take a closer
look at my life, I may decide to make
some changes. But I know that no amount of change in
the outer can truly satisfy my soul, because what I am
longing for is God.

God is the answer to every longing of my mind
and spirit! Only God can fill that special place within
because only God can call me higher. Only God can
give me the experiences that lead to new growth and
understanding.

So I seek God in all that I do. I look past appearances
and take time to see the divine order that I know is
inherent within each situation. As I seek to know more
of God, my soul is nurtured. The more God is in my life,
the greater satisfaction I receive from everything I do.

**"O God, you are my God, I seek you."
—Psalm 63:1**

Day 341

—◆—

Thank You, God, for creating me!

GOD CREATED ME

I may or may not celebrate my birthday each year, but each new day is reason enough to celebrate the gift of life, the gift of God's spirit within me!

Through the spirit of God within, I have the ability to achieve anything I desire to achieve. With God, nothing is impossible, nothing can keep me from experiencing the joy and fulfillment that God created me to experience.

Although I may go through what seems to be a failure, I know that it can be a valuable learning experience that urges me further along the path. So I celebrate this experience and give thanks for what it has taught me about life.

I grow in spiritual awareness as I let God show me what life can be. "Thank You, God, for Your wonderful gift of life!"

"To the thirsty I will give water as a gift from the spring of the water of life."
—Revelation 21:6

Day 342

—◆—

Today and every day, I honor God's presence.

HONORING YOU

God, thank You for life and for Your presence in my life. You are the best friend I could ever have—my confidant, my guide.

I feel Your unconditional love for me as if it were a gentle whisper of the wind washing over me. I look at my loved ones and feel such joy, for I see Your glory and majesty reflected on their faces.

I honor Your greatness by living my life totally centered in You. You are in me, and I am a part of You.

You are my Alpha and my Omega, and through You I will always know oneness and eternal life. I commit my life to You, for You are the One who molded me in Your image and gave me life.

God, today and every day, I honor Your presence.

"You guide me with your counsel,
and afterward you will receive me with honor."
—Psalm 73:24

Day 343

—◆—

The Spirit of life is expressing through me now!

SPIRIT OF LIFE

I hold on to my faith, my hope, my healing and do not waste any energy on concern. My energy is directed to my body's capacity to heal.

Right now, just as I am, I am a magnificent creation of an ever-present, all-providing Creator. As I bless my body with thoughts of healing, I send a message of life and renewal to every cell and organ.

I know that I can never be separated from the presence of God because I am eternally one with the Creator. I may sense that a healing is taking place instantly or over time, but the marvel of a healing is beyond timing and sensing.

I am one of God's creations of life, and as such I know that the Spirit of life is expressing through me now!

" 'I can see people, but they look like trees, walking.' Then
Jesus laid his hand on his eyes again . . .
and his sight was restored."
—Mark 8:24–25

Day 344

—◆—

*I gently still my thoughts and
experience the loving presence of God.*

**DIVINE
MAJESTY**

I may not know what the future
holds for me, but I do know that in the
unknown something familiar is waiting
for me: God is always there. Wherever
I go, God's spirit is within me and goes before me.

By stilling my thoughts and feeling the loving presence
of God, I quell any fears of the unknown.

God will never forsake me. The same God that is
powerful enough to have created the sun, the moon,
and the stars of the universe and to have sent mighty
rivers surging across the ground to forge immense
canyons is still gentle enough to have created the delicate
petals of a fragile flower and loving enough to have
created me.

How can I not feel awed and blessed and perfectly
safe when I consider that I am a part of such beauty
and majesty?

> **"My presence will go with you,
> and I will give you rest."**
> **—Exodus 33:14**

Day 345

—◆—

God is my greatest blessing, the originator of all that blesses me.

GREATEST BLESSING Whatever my need or desire, I know that God is with me and is the source of lasting happiness and joy.

If I need healing, I trust in God and know that God is filling my body with healing life. Divine life alters every condition so that my body can express more of the divine life within.

Do I wish for guidance or peace? Then I turn to God with the desires of my heart, and God will fill me with the light which shines so brightly that all darkness is cast away.

If I need help with my financial situation, again I let God help me by filling my mind with ideas that I can act upon to turn my life around.

I let go of any concern and know that God is my greatest blessing.

> **"I am going to bring . . . recovery and healing;**
> **I will heal them and reveal to them abundance**
> **of prosperity and security."**
> **—Jeremiah 33:6**

Day 346

——◆——

The spirit of God keeps me forever young and accomplishing more.

FOREVER YOUNG

As a child, I probably could not wait until I was grown up and on my own. And then I found that there is no magic age when I stop learning and discovering.

Well, the reality of it all is that I am forever young, forever a child who is growing, learning, and discovering every day—no matter how many years I have invested in growing up.

And that is good news! Each day I am given fresh opportunities with which I can stretch beyond the goals I reached the day before. I am continually increasing my awareness of myself as a child of God, a child who is not limited by age or experience.

The spirit of God within me keeps me forever young in heart and keeps me growing and accomplishing more.

> "It is that very Spirit bearing witness with
> our spirit that we are children of God,
> and if children, then heirs."
> —Romans 8:16–17

Day 347

——◆——

My faith is a growing belief in the power of God in me and in my world.

GROWING FAITH

Sometimes a challenge may come up suddenly as if a raging storm is overtaking me. What do I do?

I remember that when Jesus and His disciples were in a storm at sea, He calmed the waters with these words: "Peace! Be still!" Then He asked the disciples a question, "Where is your faith?" which was an awakening call of faith in God for the disciples. And this same timeless message of faith reaches out to me now.

Where is my faith today? I put my faith in the power of God within me and within my world. If there is a storm cloud of controversy or inharmony threatening the peace of my life, I remember to say, "Peace! Be still!" and to have faith in the power of God to bring me safely through.

"He woke up and rebuked the wind and the raging waves; they ceased, and there was a calm."
—Luke 8:24

Day 348

$\diamond$

I am a light of God's goodwill in a world aglow with harmony.

GOODWILL God, You are the one source of goodwill that shines in and through each person willing to be a light of peace. And, God, I am willing to let Your goodwill shine out from me to greet each person I meet and to light the way of peace and harmony.

I live in harmony with a diverse and wondrous world of Your creation. I can do this because I am one with You, the source of goodwill that lights up the world.

I bring the light of love and understanding with me wherever I go. I let Your goodwill shine brightly in my home, my workplace, my neighborhood.

Loving words, total acceptance, and gentle actions are just a few of the wonders that Your goodwill sparks into action in person after person so that the world glows with harmony.

> **"Live in harmony with one another."**
> **—Romans 12:16**

Day 349

—◆—

*I am on a journey of life and
discovery with God as my guide.*

**M Y
G U I D E**
One thing I know: With God as my
guide, I am moving forward in my
journey, no matter what path I am on
right now.

Whether I am on an uphill path or coasting downhill,
I am on my right path because God is my guide. On my
journey, I will experience both the challenge of the
climb and the elation of being at the mountaintop. All
experiences are points of interest along the way from
which I gain strength, stamina, and understanding.

If I stumble, God is there to take me by the hand and
steady me so that I can continue my walk. And I meet
many people—some of whom will share a journey of a
lifetime with me and some only a brief stroll. But we
each give and receive the rich companionship of the
children of a loving, caring God.

**"You hold my right hand.
You guide me with your counsel."
—Psalm 73:23–24**

Day 350

---◆---

*Oh, how beautiful, God, is the
assurance of Your love and peace!*

**BLESSED
ASSURANCE**

My times in prayer stir up peace
within me that nourishes me with
serenity even in the most stressful
times. How beautiful is the assurance
of God's love and peace in every moment of my life!

Each prayer is a reunion of my conscious awareness
with the presence of God. Each time I reach a total
awareness of God, I feel a surge of peace. And the
beauty of it all is that God is always present in me and
in my life.

Allowing the healing, soothing flow of peace to roll
over me, I relax and discover new energy and creativity.
I am amazed that what seemed like such a challenge
only moments before I prayed has been replaced by
my understanding of a solution all in a moment of
peaceful prayer.

**"How beautiful upon the mountains
are the feet of the messenger who announces peace."
—Isaiah 52:7**

Day 351

—◆—

God's presence is with me always.

DIVINE PRESENCE There is a presence with me right now and in every moment of my life. I may not be able to see this divine presence, but God is with me. And the marvelous effects of God's greatness are far reaching.

No matter if I were to move from one side of the room to another or from one side of the world to the other, God's presence would still be with me, protecting me and loving me.

I take a deep breath and know that I am breathing in divinity. I feel the earth beneath my feet and know that I am touching the haven that God gave to all.

And because God takes the care to see that my needs are met, that I have air to breathe and food to eat, how can I not feel the protecting presence of God with me at all times? God's presence is with me now—and always.

"I am with you always."
—Matthew 28:20

Day 352

—◆—

I enter into God's kingdom through the gates of prayer.

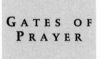

GATES OF PRAYER

When I turn within during my times of contemplation and meditation, I am entering through the gates of prayer into a sanctuary where I can relax in a comfort that only God can give.

As I pass through the gates of prayer, I pause for a moment and bask in the glow of pure love and unconditional support. I feel God's loving presence so completely that I immediately give thanks.

In this moment, I know with new understanding and appreciation that God is my strength and assurance. God gives to me with unconditional love, and I give complete faith and wholehearted love in return.

In the kingdom within, God alone waits for me. Nothing is required of me but to be in the silence, for I am one with God. The love and joy I feel transcend any need for words.

"Enter his gates with thanksgiving."
—Psalm 100:4

Day 353

—◆—

*Through my oneness with God,
possibilities become reality.*

**JUST
IMAGINE**

I can imagine a world where people
are united in spirit and in love. And by
attuning myself to the power of God, I
can do more than imagine it—I can
live it!

Through God's spirit within me, I can love those
who seem to be unlovable, understand what looks to
be unexplainable, and reach the seemingly unattainable.

Divine spirit is expressed by me as peace and love,
faith and hope. And if others doubt the possibility of
my envisioned world of united faith, I rest in the knowledge that God is guiding me.

Through my oneness with God, possibilities become
more than just things I dream about—they become
probabilities, and with time and concentration on my
part, those probabilities become reality.

> **"Keep on doing the things that you have learned
> and received and heard and seen in me,
> and the God of peace will be with you."**
> **—Philippians 4:9**

Day 354

—◆—

*I am fulfilled in life as a beloved
child of God.*

FULFILLED Speaking the above words stirs up great self-assurance and strength within me. To repeat them and honestly believe in my mind and heart that they are true takes courage and faith.

But I can say them and know them to be true because I have not only self-assurance, but also God-assurance. My faith tells me that God does not judge me but does rely on me to be the best child of God that I can be.

Stepping stones in the past led me to today, but nothing in the past or the present can take away the spiritual oneness and understanding that I have gained.

So whether I say this affirmation today, tomorrow, or next year, I will always know it to be true. God and I are one, and I am totally aware and comfortable with who I am.

I am fulfilled in life, for I am a beloved child of God.

"Know that I am with you."
—Genesis 28:15

Day 355

—◆—

God, I give thanks that You are my refuge and my constant companion.

MY REFUGE I may have had times when I changed my plans because of a sudden, unexplainable thought. And that change in plans changed my whole life. Only afterward did I understand that with this thought, God was showing me a better way.

"O God, I do take refuge in You. My heart soars because Your spirit is everywhere. I am free to move and travel, knowing that I am never beyond Your care and protection. Whatever I plan and wherever I go, I listen for Your guidance, knowing that even the gentlest of promptings can lead me to wonderful new discoveries.

"The more I give thanks to You and include You in my thoughts, plans, and time, the more aware I am that You are my refuge and constant companion."

**"Protect me, O God, for in you I take refuge . . .
You show me the path of life."
—Psalm 16:1, 11**

Day 356

—◆—

God sustains and enlivens me with the breath of life.

BREATH OF LIFE

The breath of life does more than refresh me physically and mentally. It attunes me to my own spirituality.

Breathing slowly and fully satisfies and soothes me, which allows my spiritual nature to come forth unimpeded.

Calm down and slowly, fully breathe in the breath of life. This is what I tell myself in any time of anxiety or confusion. Then I do it. As I breathe slowly, gently, and fully of the breath of life, the spirit of God sustains me.

I know beyond a shadow of a doubt that I face nothing alone because God gives me life and sustains my life. I also know that in every moment of every day, God's spirit of life and wisdom enlivens and guides me. Thank You, God!

**"The spirit of God has made me,
and the breath of the Almighty gives me life."
—Job 33:4**

Day 357

—◆—

I awaken to my true self by remembering that
God holds me in high esteem.

REMEMBER   If ever thoughts of being unloved or unlovable, of being incapable or undeserving come to mind, I remember how God sees me. God holds me in such high esteem, how can I think anything less of myself? How can I act as if I am anyone else but the loved and capable person I am?

Remembering that I am loved by and precious to God brings out the best in me. And when I think or interact with others, I know that they are precious and loved by God, too. When I look at others and remember they are sacred creations of God, I can do no less than love and hold them in high esteem as well.

Yes, I remember that we are all loved by God and precious to God, and in that remembering I discover the true joy of spirit.

> **"You are precious in my sight,**
> **and honored, and I love you."**
> **—Isaiah 43:4**

Day 358

—◆—

I am one with God in a union of spirit, life, and love.

UNION WITH GOD

Loving Spirit, teach me to do Your will. Guide my steps and show me how to bring more of Your light into my world.

Your loving presence fills me with all the love, light, and life I will ever need. Attuned to You, I am so aware of the blessings that each day offers.

You are in me, and I am in You. Our union is of the spirit, and Your presence is in every cell of my body and in the very air that I breathe.

I know how it feels to be truly alive as You live in me, love through me, and use me as an instrument of blessings for others.

O loving Spirit, I surrender to You and gladly listen for the sweet inspiration that You pour out to me. My soul sings with joy, for I know now, more than ever before, that it is Your presence within me that gives me true happiness and lasting peace.

"The Father and I are one."
—John 10:30

Day 359

—◆—

I am a precious, spiritual being of light and life.

SPIRITUAL BEING   I am always eager to meet a person who is, in truth, a spiritual being—one with unlimited strengths, incredible wisdom, and abundant creativity.

Well, I have only to look at my own reflection to see this person. I need only speak with my own voice to hear this person and bring my hand to my face to touch this person.

I am God's glorious creation, and because I am, the power of the Almighty responds to my call and the intelligence of the universe rushes to my aid. I have all the love and comfort I could ever hope to have within me. Yet there is more.

If ever I forget who I am, I watch and listen, for God works in mysterious and wonderful ways to let me know of my sacredness and the sacredness of all creation.

> "So God created humankind in his image,
> in the image of God he created them."
> —Genesis 1:27

Day 360

—◆—

I honor the presence of God within me and within every person.

HONOR GOD   Every time I am kind or caring, loving or understanding toward another, I honor God, for I honor the presence of God within that person and within me.

When I think of all the people who serve God through the work that they do and through the care that they give, I am honored to belong to the family of God.

The caregivers of our world are on call day and night. They answer the call for help, the need for peace, and the desire for companionship. The care that they give is a holy activity, whether it is given to family, friends, or strangers. In fact, caregivers are loving people who never meet a stranger, for they recognize all people for whom they truly are—members of the family of God.

**"And the king will answer them,
'Truly I tell you, just as you did it to one of the least
of these who are members of my family,
you did it to me.' "
—Matthew 25:40**

Day 361

—◆—

By following the Golden Rule, I become a good shepherd to myself and others.

GOOD SHEPHERD

"In everything do to others as you would have them do to you." This is the Golden Rule that Jesus taught and lived, and what better guide can I follow than the one given by the Master Teacher?

As I follow the Golden Rule, I find that I just naturally act more loving and kind. I form a heart-and-soul connection with others because I am acting from the divine Presence within us. I am taking on the sacred role of being God's good shepherd of love for the whole world.

The good shepherd acts as a caring, guiding presence, a calming influence in any storm. As God's good shepherd, I convey a message of hope and goodwill, a message of love and understanding which lets the world know that I care.

**"I am the good shepherd. I know my own and my own know me, just as the Father knows me."
—John 10:14–15**

Day 362

—◆—

I am on a mission of divine discovery!

DIVINE MISSION People have often searched for excitement and adventure, finding mountains to climb, oceans to cross, and frontiers to conquer.

But I know of a far greater journey that beckons me, so I follow an urging which leads me on a magnificent discovery of the spirit of God that dwells within me.

Mine is a holy mission, a mission that will change my life forever. I move forward with strength of mind and assurance, for I am fulfilling an inner quest that can no longer be denied. Spirit is calling me to explore the infinite possibilities that are available to me, and I answer that call with faith.

My mission is an inner journey home to God. In the silence of my soul, God waits for me. I have taken no physical steps forward, but I have made a tremendous leap of faith on a mission of divine discovery!

"For with you is the fountain of life."
—Psalm 36:9

Day 363

—◆—

*I am a living, breathing miracle
of life.*

**HEALED
AND
WHOLE**

A healing may seem miraculous, even when I understand that I was created with the ongoing, healing life of God within me. Out of my reverence for the sacredness of life, I feel such gratitude in being healed.

The truth is that I am an amazing creation of life, so I never underestimate the life of God within me to continually heal me. I know that the love of God heals me and frees me of any memory or experience that would control or limit me. I rejoice that the spirit of God comforts me no matter what I am going through.

Healing may seem like a miracle, but *I* am no less a miracle. So I rest in the healing presence of God—always with me, always within me. I am healed and whole.

> "The crowd was amazed when they saw the mute speaking, the maimed whole, the lame walking, and the blind seeing. And they praised the God of Israel."
> —Matthew 15:31

Day 364

—◆—

*My goal is to let God bring out
the best in me.*

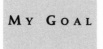

MY GOAL

Every day, I want to be the best I can be—whether my role is as a parent or a child, an employee or a supervisor, a musician or an artist. But I am not in competition with others. My goal is to be *my* best, to give *my* best. And when communication with God is my first goal, everything else gently settles into place.

"God, yesterday is gone, so I release any regrets about what I did or did not do and move on to a fresh new day. Thank You for giving me another chance to be even better today.

"The anticipation of letting Your love shine through me, Your wisdom enlighten my thoughts, and Your life enliven me fills me and thrills me. I realize that this is the best I can do, the best anyone can do."

**"They are to do good, to be rich in good works,
generous, and ready to share, thus storing up
for themselves the treasure of a good foundation
for the future."
—1 Timothy 6:18**

Day 365

—◆—

Being at peace and expressing peace are ways I bless the whole world.

WORLD PEACE

What can one person like me do that would be felt and cherished throughout the world? I can be at peace in my own part of the world and express peace to the whole world.

Peace begins within each individual. So my peaceful thoughts, words, and actions reach out from me to every woman and man, every child and animal, and every neighborhood and country of the world.

As the peace I express joins with the peace expressed by others around the world, I begin to understand the blessedness of giving that Jesus spoke about and lived in his own life.

Peace is more than thoughts, words, and actions. It is also a spiritual awareness that reaches out from me to touch the soul of the world.

"Peace I leave with you; my peace I give to you."
—John 14:27

ABOUT THE EDITOR

Editor-in-chief of *Daily Word* magazine since 1985, Colleen Zuck was previously editor-in-chief of *Wee Wisdom*, the world's oldest continually published children's magazine.

Colleen is a popular speaker among the *Daily Word* community in the United States and internationally, where people are drawn to her warm, genuine graciousness. In addition to her editorial work, which she says is her life's passion, Colleen enjoys gardening and her many and diverse pets.

AN INVITATION

Daily Word is the magazine of Silent Unity, a worldwide prayer ministry now in its second century of service. Silent Unity believes that:

- ◆ *all people are sacred*
- ◆ *God is present in all situations*
- ◆ *everyone is worthy of love, peace, health, and prosperity*

Silent Unity prays with all who ask for prayer. Every prayer request is held in absolute confidence, and there is never a charge. You are invited to contact Silent Unity 24 hours a day, any day of the year.

Write: Silent Unity, 1901 NW Blue Parkway,
Unity Village, MO 64065-0001
Or call: (816) 246-5400 fax: (816) 251-3554
Online: http://www.unityworldhq.org

THERE'S MORE!

If you enjoy these inspirational messages, you may wish to subscribe to *Daily Word* magazine and receive a fresh, contemporary, uplifting message for each day of the month. With its inclusive, universal language, this pocket-size magazine is a friend to millions of people around the world.

For subscription information regarding *Daily Word* in English (regular and large-type editions) or in Spanish, please write:

Silent Unity, 1901 NW Blue Parkway,
Unity Village, MO 64065-0001
Or call: 1-800-669-0282 fax: (816) 251-3554
Online: http://www.dailyword.org

INDEX

INDEX